GW00363013

SUSSE
MEMORABILIA

A COLLECTOR'S PRICE GUIDE

Sandy Hernu

S.B. Publications

By the Same Author

Exploring Alfriston and The Cuckmere Valley
East Sussex Walks (Brighton, Eastbourne and Lewes area)
East Sussex Walks (In and around the Rural Villages)
East Sussex Walks (Exploring 1066 Country)
West Sussex Walks (Arundel, Steyning and Worthing Area)
Secrets of East Sussex
Secrets of West Sussex
'Q' - The Biography of Desmond Llewelyn

First published in 2002 by S.B. Publications
19 Grove Road, Seaford, East Sussex BN25 1TP
Tel: 01323 893498

© Sandy Hernu

No part of this publication may be reproduced, stored in a retrieval system
or transmitted by any means without the prior permission of the
copyright holder or publisher.

ISBN 1 85770 265 4

Designed and Typeset by EH Graphics, East Sussex (01273) 515527
Printed by Pageturn Ltd, East Sussex, BN3 7EG. Tel: (01273) 821500

CONTENTS

ACKNOWLEDGMENTS

S.A.Benz. c/o SB Publications, 19 Grove Road, Seaford. BN25 1TP 01323 893498 - **(Badges)**.

Newhaven Maritime Museum (Curator - Peter Bailey). Paradise Leisure Park, Avis Road. Newhaven BN9 0DH - **(Maritime)**.

The Parker Pen Company. 52 Railway Road, Newhaven. BN9 0AU - **(Parker Pens)**.

Antonia Raine. Desk Top items. 0208 688 3935 - **(Parker Pens)**.

Mrs. P. Clarke. - **(Parker Pens)**.

Anne of Cleves House Museum. 52 Southover High Street, Lewes. BN7 1YE. 01273 474610 - **(Wealden Iron and Pottery)**.

Margaret and Richard Buss. 01323 843845 - **(Dicker Ware)**.

David Back. 20th century Ceramics. 01273 845791 or 07974 810692 - **(Pottery)**.

Tarquin Cole. Rye Pottery, Ferry Road, Rye. TN31 7DH. 01797 223038 - **(Rye Pottery)**.

Cornfield Antiques Centre. 18 Cornfield Terrace, Eastbourne. BN21 4NS. 01323 733345 - **(Pottery and General Collectables)**.

Churchill Antiques & Collectors Market. 20 Sackville Road, Bexhill-on-Sea. 01424 733355 - **(Crested China, Pottery and general Collectables)**.

Judges' Postcards Ltd. 176 Bexhill Road, St Leonards-on-Sea. TN38 8BN. 01424 420919 - **(Judges' Postcards)**.

Roger Davis. The Sussex Ephemera Society. 01903 241503 - **(Brighton Ephemera)**.

George and Deirdre Stevens. The Boxroom, Old Needlemakers, West Street, Lewes. - **(General Collectables)**.

The Regimental Military Museum. The Redoubt Fortress, Eastbourne. - **(The Royal Sussex Regiment)**.

The Last Post (Militaria). The Barn Collectors, Seaford. 01323 898551 - **(The Royal Sussex Regiment)**.

Glyndebourne Opera House (Archives), Lewes. 01273 812321 - **(Glyndebourne Opera)**.

Eastbourne Antiques Market. 80 Seaside, Eastbourne. 01323 642233 - **(General Collectables)**.

Gorringes Auctions, incorporating Julian Dawson. 15 North Street, Lewes. BN7 2PD. 01273 472503 - **(General Collectables)**.

Carol Turrell - **(Collectable Ceramics)**.

HOW TO USE THIS BOOK

This comprehensive guide is designed to give 'at-a-glance' information on Sussex Memorabilia. Simply go to the Contents page to find your area of interest and then turn to the page that has the required heading. This will begin with general information and history on the subject which is followed by a pictorial price section on the same. But please note. This book should not be used for valuations; it is essentially a price guide and reflects the prices asked or realised by a variety of Antique outlets across the county.

A white glazed pottery pitcher marked 'MH' 9¹/₂ ins (24 cms) high. £5 - 6

A 20th century white terracotta jug decorated with a blue/green/yellow floral pattern. From a pottery at Amberley. 8 ins (20 cms) high. £5 - 6

A late 20th century terracotta jug with a creamy glazed rim marked 'Gopsall'. 6¹/₂ ins (16.5 cms) high. £5 - 6

Description
A brief outline of the item pictured generally giving some of the following: medium, colour, date, maker, measurements and, very occasionally, condition.

Price Guide
From the lowest to the highest, the price guides referring to each item have been found at Auctions, Antique Shops, Antique & Collectables Markets and Fairs, as well as Private Collections. Condition naturally affects the price substantially, as can the locality and/or current trend.

A Rodmell pottery dish. 8 ins (20 cms) long. £4 - 5

Terracotta pot marked 'Chappell' 5¹/₂ ins (14 cms) high. £4 - 5

A highly glazed white mug decorated with a blue and green fish. JCJ Pottery. 4 ins (10 cms) high £1.50 - 2.00

Please note that some of the collectables on this page are still being produced and the items shown reflect only their second-hand value.

Additional Facts
The boxed text covers any extra information applicable to that particular page.

c. 1990's. A decorative stoneware wall pot from a pottery at Crawley. 5 ins (12.5 cms) high £5 - 6

Newick Pottery jug. 4¹/₂ ins (11.5 cms) high. £8 - 10

A textured Hastings Pottery plant pot. 6 ins (15 cms) high £12 - 14

AROUND SUSSEX
An Introduction to Collecting Local Memorabilia

Over the last two decades the interest in collectables has multiplied. The growth of Antique Markets, Antique Fairs, Boot Fairs, Jumble Sales and Auctions all offer those with a discerning eye for a bargain, the chance to build a worthwhile collection. However, just what to collect can sometimes be a problem. Sussex Memorabilia is the first price guide to provide an insight into some of the county's own past, present and future treasures and gives exciting, as well as lucrative, ideas on which to base a collection.

A walk down every High Street could offer inspiration. Take note of the once familiar shops that have disappeared, literally overnight. Shop memorabilia, which includes signs, advertising, packaging and even old bills (see Brighton Ephemera), can give an in-depth picture of the changing face of trading. Local businesses such as the Sussex County Building Society, Achille Serre Dry Cleaners, John Beal Stationers or, more recently, Hanningtons, that much loved Brighton department store, have closed forever or merged with larger companies.

A Victorian mahogany circular dial wall timepiece inscribed 'Hanningtons – Brighton' with an estimated price of £300 – 400.

Shop memorabilia can be big business and a classic example of this occurred when the residual contents of Hanningtons were auctioned in 2001. Amid frenzied bidding the store's solid and simple timepiece, with an intrinsic value of around £300 to £400 fetched a staggering £2,400 simply because it had 'Hanningtons' emblazoned across the face.

A small brass door knocker depicting the clock on the tower of Rye Church. 6 ins x 3 ins (15 cms x 7½ cms) £10 - 14

Some enthusiasts base their collection around historical buildings such as Chichester Cathedral, The Royal Pavilion, one or more of the Sussex castles, priories or churches. There's Jack Fuller's Follies, which originally included Belle Tout Lighthouse; the great manor houses like Firle, Parham or Glyndebourne, (see Glyndebourne Opera). Or what about artefacts linked to seaside resorts boasting places of interest; for example, piers, bandstands, the net shops at Hastings or The De La Warr Pavilion in Bexhill.

The many Sussex-based industries, both past and present, have naturally produced a wealth of collectables. Most have had humble beginnings such as the Potteries in Rye (see Pottery), or Thomas Smith trugs at Herstmonceux, whose slatted wooden baskets came in all sizes for agricultural or household purposes. It was only after Thomas Smith won a Gold Medal at the Great Exhibition at Crystal Palace in 1851 and

A simple garden trug 18 ins x 10 ins (46 cms x 25½ cms) £20 - 30

subsequently a large order for trugs from Queen Victoria, that the business began to flourish. Today, trugs are still made at Herstmonceux but the older baskets can often be found filled with dried flowers and gracing the displays in Antique Markets. These usually fetch anything from £20 to £70 for an unusual example.

Baxters, the Victorian publishers and printers were based in Lewes and here George Baxter, eldest son of John Baxter, was born in 1804. After schooling and learning the art of wood engraving in London, George returned to work in his father's printing works. During the next few years he started to experiment with the process of printing in oil colours using wood and metal blocks. These experiments proved fruitful and he went on to produce a wide range of colour prints which are now highly sought after and known as 'Baxter Prints'. However, take care when buying. The prints fade or mark easily and this affects the value.

A Baxter print showing some damage and depicting a view of Lewes from South Street. £30 - 40

There are of course many other local industries whose products and related ephemera arouse interest amongst collectors. These are the names of a few: - Shippams Paste, Chichester; McDougals Flour, whose premises were at Horsebridge Mill, Horsebridge, from 1921 until 1969; Caffyns Garages have had branches in Sussex since the beginning of the 20th century; Harvey's Brewery in Lewes, Merrydown Cider in Horam and King and Barnes at Horsham are sources of brewery memorabilia. The Body Shop at Littlehampton could provide an up and coming collectables market in cosmetics complete with their packaging.

Sport of some sort is usually fairly high in most people's lists of part-time pursuits and a collection of memorabilia that represent a favourite game will add another enjoyable dimension. Sussex can boast a well-known link with several sports. For example, international tennis is played at Devonshire Park, Eastbourne; there's the county's very own Brighton and Hove Albion Football Club: horse racing is held at Goodwood and Plumpton to name but a few local racecourses. And apart from the Sussex County Cricket Club, cricket has a special connection for a business at Robertsbridge called Gray Nicholls. This company has produced some of the choicest bats in the world and these were once used by that famous cricketer, W.G.Grace, who declared "There were none finer". Always highly desirable, just about anything goes with sporting memorabilia from boots to caps, tickets to trophies, or bats and balls. And don't forget a well-known signature on the relative item bumps up the price.

Book worms could keep an eye open for first editions, signed copies or old local books (see Sussex Books), when searching the shelves of Charity Shops for something to read. During the 19th/20th centuries it would appear many authors, captivated by Sussex, made their homes amid its glorious scenery. Amongst the most famous were Hilaire Belloc, whose books are often associated with the county and lived at King's Land, the house adjacent to Shipley Mill, Shipley. H.G.Wells lived at Uppark, South Harting; Henry James at Lamb House, Rye; Rudyard Kipling eventually settled at Batemans on the fringes of Burwash; Lord Alfred Tennyson at Aldworth House, Blackdown, whilst the ancestral home of Percy Bysshe Shelley was the lovely Georgian mansion, Field Place, near Warnham. A.A.Milne of 'Winnie the Pooh' fame moved to Cotchfield Farm, Hartfield in 1925 and now, apart from his books, much of the early 'Poohphanalia' is collectable in its own right. John Galsworthy, author of the 'Forsyte Saga', lived at Bury House, Bury and the well-known Bloomsbury writer, Virginia Woolf, moved to Monk's House, Rodmell in 1919 having stayed regularly in Sussex since 1911.

Celebrity autographs are definitely worth collecting, particularly if it is

Desmond Llewelyn – An autograph by the man best known for his role as 'Q' in the 007 films. £50 - 70

a signed photograph or similar item of interest rather than on a blank sheet of paper. In this instance, it's anybody who is somebody in entertainment, politics or the arts and has an association with Sussex. There's the famous film actor turned author, Dirk Bogarde, whose enchanting autobiographies on his childhood in Alfriston captured readers' hearts. Laurence Olivier and Vivien Leigh, Harold Macmillan, Denis Healey, Paul McCartney and Desmond Llewelyn, better known as 'Q' of the James Bond films are a tiny handful of the celebrities who have or had a home in the county.

Souvenirs of significant events and places have been made in every conceivable material and shape since the 18th century. Sussex is no

A silver teaspoon bearing an enamelled Sussex crest. 4¹/₂ ins (11 cms) long. £15 - 20

exception. Small items in silver, wood, metal or china often bore a picture of a local scene, sometimes with either a description or 'A Present from .....', or alternatively the town crest (see also Crested China).

Undoubtedly there are endless possibilities for collecting Sussex Memorabilia but perhaps one of the most popular is postcards, maybe because they don't take up too much storage space and they're relatively inexpensive to buy. This together with the bonus of the seaside resorts meant companies, large and small, have produced a huge variety of Sussex postcards since the beginning of the 20th century. (See Judges' Postcards). Today, specialist postcard shops as well as fairs and auctions occur regularly across the county and these are well worth a visit.

A small plate marking the event of the 'Athena B' running aground on Brighton Beach after a storm in 1980. 4¹/₂ ins (12 cms) diameter. £6 - 8

Pictures by local artists, scenes, prints and maps of Sussex are always sought after and so are collections of that old favourite, The Sussex County Magazine, but only in good condition.

And last but not least and by no means all, there's shipping (see Maritime) and Railway Memorabilia. The Sussex train network started in the mid-1840's with the opening of the London Brighton and South Coast Railway. Secondary lines, like the Mid-Sussex, were completed in the latter half of the 19th century, including the Bluebell Line in 1882. This particular line which ran from East Grinstead to just north of Lewes and provided a link to the main line fell, like others, under Beeching's axe in 1958. Shortly after, the Bluebell Railway Preservation Society re-opened a stretch of track which is today a successful tourist attraction. There's no doubt, collectors of Railwayana are a highly dedicated bunch and the memorabilia does not come cheaply. Even so, whether you decide to collect Railwayana, Pottery, Ephemera or just put together a general collection to illustrate Sussex, the challenge of looking for a bargain is more than half the fun.

Incidentally, one of the best sources for any antique dealer, collector or mildly interested browser is the Ardingly Antiques Fair. This enjoyable two-day indoor/outdoor event is held six times a year at the South of England Showground at Ardingly. There are also smaller one day fairs held, again at the showground, on a Sunday. For dates and information check the press or alternatively contact the Tourist Information Centre in Horsham. 01403 211661.

BADGES

Badges are easy to produce, cheap to buy and fun to collect. They also notch up a lasting memory of people, places and events; from royalty to pop: religion to politics: sport to theatre, or simply trendy messages and current fads. Apart from photographs or postcards, there is no other item of inexpensive memorabilia that provides such a broad insight into our social history.

Badges, however, are not just a product of today's throw-away society, but have been in existence since Victorian times. Known as 'Button Badges', they were initially made from celluloid and tin on a button machine. These early examples were somewhat inferior to those simultaneously crafted in metal and enamel, which took much longer to make and often resembled a brooch. Both are now highly prized by serious collectors.

A Space badge marking an event in Brighton organised by the British Interplanetary Society. October 1987. £1 – 2.

The first badge manufacturers were American. Production in this country began around 1902, shortly after the celebrations of Queen Victoria's Diamond Jubilee and, subsequently, Edward VII's Coronation had taken place. For both these events thousands of commemorative badges had to be imported from America, and one would guess that British button manufacturers suddenly realised the potential of the badge market.

Although the boom years of badges were undoubtedly during the1960's and 70's, this form of descriptive art is still extremely popular and, as always, the wearers are mainly children or the youth. Collecting them however seems to transcend those parameters and there are now several badge organisations to support this growing hobby. Pre-war badges are particularly sought after and one of those controversial Gollies or a Butlins badge can fetch £20 – 30.

An unusual Morris Men badge with the Long Man of Wilmington in the background. £1 – 1.50p

As you don't need to be a millionaire to collect the majority of post-war badges, car boot sales, jumble sales and flea markets are good places to start searching; so too are charity shops. And finally, if you're wondering how something can become collectable when it's so plentiful and cheap to buy in the first place, therein lies your answer. Most badges – probably more than 90% of them – end up in the dustbin and leave the few that remain to become something of a rarity.

Nine assorted Museum badges from the 1970's onwards. *50p - £2*

Badges from seven Sussex Wildlife attractions. *50p - £1.50*

Seven 'travel' badges from the 1980's onwards. *£1 - 3*

Four badges from Drusillas Zoo spanning (from far right) approximately sixty years. **£1 - 4**

Two late 20th century Father Christmas badges. **50p - £1.50**

c.1970's. Three assorted badges depicting The Pier, Brighton, the Lighthouse at Beachy Head and St. Clement's Caves, Hastings (some damage). **£1 - 2**

Seven badges showing various places in Sussex. **50p - £1.50**

Three badges from former Sussex Building Societies, now merged with the national building societies. **£1 - 2**

c.1970's. Four badges from Sussex attractions. **£2 - 4**

BOTTLE COLLECTING

Sifting through the garbage of yesteryear could hardly be described as fun, yet for the rare few, grovelling through long decayed debris for undiscovered treasure, it represents Utopia. In spite of icy winds or driving rain, digging for old bottles is like a drug – addictive, and inclement conditions are ignored. The feeling of euphoria on unearthing a perfect stoneware bottle (which probably hasn't seen the light of day for a hundred years) is likened by one collector to 'opening the Christmas stocking' of one's childhood.

The rumblings of interest in Victorian bottles began in a calm enough fashion in the 1950's. Not just in Sussex but across the country, rural areas were urbanised and in the process bygone rubbish tips were excavated to make way for progress. Some of the artefacts discovered in these tips aroused a mild curiosity amongst the 'collector' fraternity. Apart from the inevitable fragments of crockery findings included pot lids (mostly black print on white), blacking pots, salt jars, tiny stoneware ink bottles, clay pipes, pottery or glass jars and, of course, bottles. These were made of stoneware or glass with impressed, printed or embossed marks and once contained a variety of household, medicinal, alcoholic and non-alcoholic products: ginger beer bottles were particularly prevalent.

c.1850. Made by Doulton Lambeth, this stoneware bottle displays the trademark of The London and Brighton Bottling Company, New England Road, Brighton and Oswin Street, London. 7 ins (18 cms) high. £120 - 140

In no time, the Bottle Collector was born and like the Gold Rush, Bottle Fever escalated. The merest whisper of a 'sighting' sent the enthusiast scurrying to the scene, often chanced upon by maintenance workers whilst repairing drains or gas pipes. The growing number of experts poured over old maps and books or contacted local authorities to establish the whereabouts of Victorian and Edwardian dumping grounds. Permission then had to be granted by the landowner for a dig to commence and, if lucrative, the site could literally be awash with bottle collectors from dawn till dusk. It's rumoured that some even brought in small earth shifting vehicles to speed up the process, but only succeeded in making themselves unpopular with everybody concerned.

By the end of the 1970's, the fever had peaked. Certainly, all the major tips in Sussex had been exhausted leaving only the village sites to be explored in a more leisurely fashion. During those last twenty years clubs, magazines, festivals and fairs had been organised to keep the enthusiast informed of events, values and current trends. Bottles were discussed, swapped, sold, advertised and re-sold. Now they had a firmly established place within the hierarchy of Antique Collectables.

Although the history of bottles goes way back into the mists of time, the golden years of production undoubtedly began in the mid-19th century, when it appeared the merits of company advertising on the package suddenly dawned. Thereafter, consumer products were sold bearing artistically commercial logos and information on coloured glass or hand thrown pottery vessels. The vivid, yet inky-blue of poison bottles which often carried the warning 'Not to be taken' are unforgettable: so too is the iridescent milky glow of highly glazed earthenware jars and pots whose lids often displayed coloured transfer printed pictures. Then there's that curiously rustic feel of salt-glazed stoneware bottles. A hundred years ago all these items were consigned to the dustbin shortly after being purchased. Now they form many a valuable collection.

From 1825 until the last war, records indicate that Sussex boasted an inordinate number of breweries and mineral water companies. Although not all in operation at the same time (some lasted a year or two and others may have been depots), it's interesting to note that if all these 'liquid factories' were added together, the total would be in excess of 750. A staggering amount but what is even more staggering is the fact that around 300 of them were situated in the Brighton area alone.

So, why Brighton as opposed to Worthing, which had only about 40 factories, or Hastings that had in the region of 50? The answer must lie with the London/Brighton railway link opened in 1841. Suddenly the gracious seaside town, host to the cream of Victorian society, became easily accessible to every Londoner. The new form of transport offered an away-day to the coast where sun, sand and sea laced with winkles, sweetmeats and ginger beer were essential ingredients. So were the taverns, one supposedly situated on every street corner. Here, the ale was pulled from stoneware containers and served in tankards to the constant stream of visitors.

Ironically, as Brighton's image as a tourist attraction grew, so the elegant stuccoed buildings of Prinny's day hid increasingly dirty streets and overcrowded alleys where drunkenness was commonplace. However, this ensured the landlords, brewers and mineral water companies prospered and also illustrates the vast quantity of bottles to be disposed of one way or another.

A Great Glen Malt Whisky jug made by Doulton. Encircling the neck are the words: Palmeira House, Brighton. 13 ins (33 cms) high.
£120 - 145

A 19th century salt-glazed flask depicting Queen Victoria. On the back is the name and address of the brewery:- Savage & Austin, The Shades, Steyne Lane, Brighton. 7¹/₂ ins (18¹/₂ cms) high. £350 – 385.

For a while Brighton used an effective if short-lived method of discarding them. Twice a week the horse drawn dustcart would pick its way through the streets and collect the empties. When it was full the horse would pull the cart up to the edge of the cliffs at Kemp Town, where it would be up-ended so the bottles fell straight into the sea. Perhaps many appeared on the next in-coming tide, for the town soon resorted to burying them in the tips sited on its outskirts.

So what does the enthusiast look for apart from the desirable piece to fill the niche in a collection? Unusually shaped flasks or bottles depicting famous people, animals or objects are always highly sought after; Queen Victoria was a popular subject; so was the unnamed 'Man on a Barrel'. There is a marvellous example of a salt-glazed fish bottle on display in Brighton Museum. Then there is the 'Sussex Pig', mainly produced by the former Bellevue Pottery at Rye. Traditionally, this was a flask with a removable head used for drinking the health of the bride and groom at their wedding. The pig's head could stand on its snout and the separate body which was used as a jug, would be inscribed with the words:-

"You can pook and you can shuv
but a Sussex Pig he wun't be druv."

Today, the digs are few and bottles are found above ground at auctions, fairs and markets for a price, rather than below ground for nothing. Most collections tend to be based on certain features. On stoneware this can include the county, the town, the brewery, a type of emblem (i.e. birds), coloured tops or the pottery (i.e. Doulton, Denby etc.). On glass it may also be the town, design, colour, embossed logo or past contents. Condition is paramount and naturally affects the value.

A 19th century Sussex pottery pig. 9¹/₂ ins. (24 cms.) long. Anne of Cleves House Museum, Lewes.

By the beginning of the 20th century, Fry & Co. had become one of the largest mineral water companies in Sussex with branches in Bexhill, Brighton, Eastbourne, Hastings and Worthing.

A fairly common bottle from R. Fry & Co. 8 ins (20 cms) high. £5 - 6

A container from Ballard & Co.Ltd. a Lewes-based brewery that had traded from 1882 to 1927. 14 ins (36 cms) high. £35 - 50

c. 1900. A large stoneware container from the brewery R. Fry & Co. Ltd. Their trademark depicts two fishes and printed below is Hastings, Brighton, Eastbourne. 13 ins (33 cms) high. £50 - 70

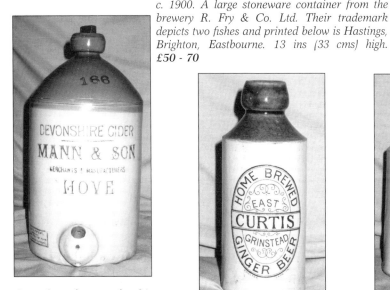

On the front of this container, Mann & Son of Hove state they were merchants and manufacturers of Devonshire cider. 14½ ins (37 cms) high. £15 - 30

A Doulton Lambeth brown topped bottle made for Curtis of East Grinstead. 7 ins (18 cms) high. £100 - 120

Two stoneware bottles simply printed with C. Beaton, Portfield, Chichester and J. Rawlins & Son. Whyke, Chichester. 7½ ins (19 cms) high. £50 - 60

A bottle found at Boots the Chemists in Eastbourne. This was the first branch to be opened in Sussex in 1904. 8 ins (20 cms) high. **£18 - 25**

A salt-glazed stoneware bottle with an impressed mark: J. L. Butcher, George Hotel, Hailsham. 7 ins (18 cms) high. **£35 - 50**

A brown glazed bottle marked Hooper Struve & Co. Ltd. c.1900. Discovered on a dig near Arundel. 7$^1/_2$ ins (19 cms) high. **£20 - 25**

A 20th century Champagne shaped bottle from the Sussex Mineral Waters Co., Brighton. 9 ins (23 cms) high. **£15 - 25**

c. 1895. An attractive bottle from the Elm Brewery, Seaford. Some damage. 7$^1/_2$ ins (19 cms) high. **£35 - 45**

A ginger beer bottle c. 1890 printed M. Ellis & Co. Oxford Place, Brighton. Below is the impressed mark of the Fulham Pottery. 6$^1/_2$ ins (17 cms) high **£70 - 90**

Displaying the collectable bird trade mark of J. Woodcock & Co., this late 19th century bottle was discovered at a disused rubbish dump near Hastings. 7 ins (18 cms) high. **£60 - 70**

An extremely rare 'blue top' bottle made by the Bourne Denby pottery for G.E. Lankester, Hastings. c. 1909. 8$^1/_2$ ins (21.5 cms) high. **£250 - 300**

A 'green top' stoneware bottle from the well-known King & Barnes brewery in Horsham. 8 ins (20.5 cms) high. **£100 – 150**

c. 1899. A brown top ginger beer bottle from Tutts of Worthing. 7¹/₂ ins (19 cms) high £70 - 80

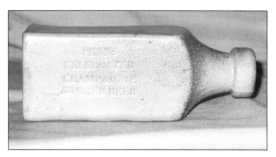

One of the very few square stoneware bottles. On the side are the impressed words: 'Penns Celebrated Champagne Ginger Beer'. 6¹/₂ ins (17 cms) high. £200 - 300

A Schilling's ginger beer bottle showing the trade mark transfer print of Brighton Pavilion. 8 ins (20.5 cms) high. £75 - 90

An example of stoneware bottle from the brewery, F R Bruce, Uckfield. Some damage. 7¹/₂ ins (19 cms) high. £30 - 40

c. 1878. A glazed brown topped bottle printed W. Lucas, Arundel and Doulton Lambeth just below the logo. 7 ins (18 cms) high. £100 - 120

Glass. Although there were several variations of the Codd Bottle, they are generally based on the original design patented by Hiram Codd in the 1870's. In principle, a Codd had two neck indentations and an internal marble. This rose when the bottle was filled with a gassy liquid to form an effective seal against the rubber washer in the neck.

Two examples of Codd bottles. c.1900 £12 - 15 each

It's uncertain if William Hamilton, producer of Soda and Mineral Water, was in fact responsible for the oval bottle known as 'The Hamilton'. Records indicate this type was in use during the late 18th century; some twenty years before Mr. Hamilton sold drink in an egg-shaped vessel.

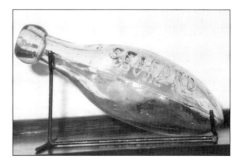

A Hamilton green glass bottle marked: Seaford £18 - 20

Rose Cold Cream from the chemists, Claisyer & Kemp, Brighton. £18 - 20

N.G.Beck (Chemist) Burgess Hill. Areca Nut Toothpaste. £20 - 24.

* By the end of the 18th century, cosmetic and savoury products had started being marketed in glazed pots, generally between 3 – 5 ins (7.5 – 12.5 cms) diameter with the relative information on the lid in a single colour. The first multi-coloured pictorial pot lid was produced by F.R. Pratt of Fenton, Staffordshire during the 1840's. Other potteries soon followed suit and these luxuriously decorated lids were hoarded even in Victorian days. However, colour was expensive to produce and the simple black on white versions, which far exceeded the colour examples in output, may not be as desirable, but are still very collectable. Prices in all cases depend on variety and condition.

Two examples of Boots Cold Cream and Boots Cherry Toothpaste sold in their chemist shops at the end of the 19th century. £18 - 20

Two Rose Cold Cream lids from the Sussex Drug Company, Brighton and F. Brooks, Queens Road, Hastings. £15 – 20 each.

Two pot lids from Hastings. J. Bell & Co's Cold Cream is complete with base. This does not add to the value greatly as it is the covers which are mainly sought after. Neve & Co. of Wellington Place claim to produce 'Saponaceous Toothpaste' – saponify being a method of converting fat into soap by treatment with alkali. £20 - 24

Cherry Toothpaste prepared by the Sussex Co-operative Drug Co. Ltd. at Brighton, Hove, Eastbourne, St.Leonards and Hastings. £15 - 18

BRIGHTON EPHEMERA

The word 'Ephemera' basically describes a paper item, printed or hand-written and required only for short-term use. As soon as the 'piece of paper' has served its purpose it is then discarded, giving therefore a scarcity value to those remaining. After all, who would have thought a 1930's petrol bill could fetch sixteen pounds; a bubble gum wrapper, sixty pounds or a 1970's film poster, six hundred pounds? In short, don't bin anything that might provide information on, say, an important event or current trend. Paper nostalgia can be worth money.

Apart from being fun and relatively inexpensive, collecting ephemera can revolve around personal interests such as sport, cooking, travel, royalty, celebrities etc. For those who are just starting, the following gives a few examples of this type of memorabilia: theatre programmes, cigarette cards, photos, postcards, autographs, letters, comics, letterheads, posters, labels, magazines, documents, greeting cards, travel tickets, sheet music and advertisements.

Some experts base their collection on a single subject: a town, a famous person, a building or a make of car. The advantages are apparent in this section on Brighton Ephemera as the printed memorabilia gradually forms a picture of the town's social history from the 19th century onwards.

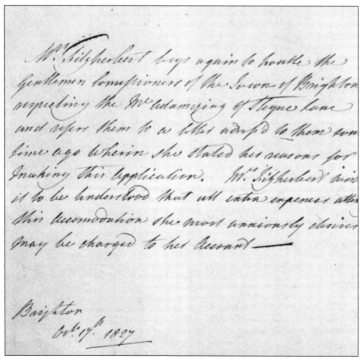

A letter written in the third person by Mrs. Fitzherbert on 17th Oct 1827 referring to Steyne Lane and addressed to 'Gentlemen Commissioners of the town of Brighton'. Mrs. Fitzherbert stayed at Steyne House, which was built for her in 1804, whenever the Prince of Wales came to the Royal Pavilion. £100 - 150

A poster warning the public that throwing stones is a dangerous offence. 1894. **£10 - 15**

A poster suggesting that under the Brighton Improvement Act 1884, street musicians are required to move on if their singing offends the neighbourhood. **£10 - 15**

An account from John Beal, a stationer, in East Street, to the Brighton Aquarium. 1972. **£15 - 20**

A poster advertising a meeting at the Town Hall in 1848. **£16 - 18**

c. 1900. A bill from Soper's Drapery Emporium once situated at the top of North Street opposite the Clock Tower. **£14 - 15**

A bill from Pegg's Royal York Hotel, Old Steyne and dated 1st February 1872. **£18 - 20**

An account from Hannington and Sons to the Brighton Aquarium dated 1879 **£20 - 25**

A luncheon bill for £2-12-0d from the Old Ship Hotel on 13th April 1885. **£13 - 15**

An 1838 bill from the Hatters, W. Fennell, in North Street. **£14 - 16**

A copy of an engraving of Brighton Railway Station. **£6 - 8**

A document containing details of the intended London to Brighton railway line. **£40 - 45**

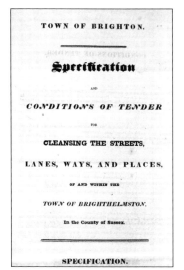

A letter from Brighton Aquarium dated 11th Sept 1906. **£10 - 15**

Detailed conditions of tender to a street cleaning contractor in 1829. **£30 - 40**

A scale of charges for the use of rooms at the Royal Pavilion in 1822. **£28 - 32**

A brochure from Du Pont's Riding School at Waterloo Street and at Norfolk Mews. **£10 - 14**

An official tramway map of Brighton. 1910. £18 - 20

A booklet on the Licensed Victuallers Protection Society of London annual excursion to Brighton and back. 1881. £22 - 25

A letter from the Eastbourne Steam Printing Works, which also had offices in Brighton, signed by J.N.Beckett, 29th May 1880. This company is now Beckett Newspapers. £14 - 18

A programme from the West Pier dated 9th October 1916 and priced at 2d. £10 - 14

A poster advertising the services of W. Hope, a fly proprietor, whose offices were at 149 North Street. c.1830. £9 - 11

An admission ticket to the Brighton Aquarium. £5 - 10

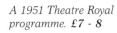

A 1951 Theatre Royal programme. £7 - 8

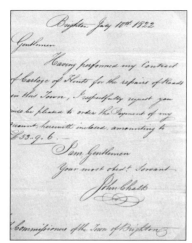

A letter to the Commissioners of the town of Brighton, dated 10th July 1882, requesting payment for a cartage of flints. £20 - 24

A photograph of the Brighton Fire Brigade c. 1900. £9 - 10

A photograph of Brighton's electricity chimney, demolished in 1929. £9 - 10

A photograph of the last Mail Coach to leave Brighton in 1905. £8 - 10

An engraving of the Baths at Brighton taken from the European Magazine. £10 - 15

A photograph of an early trolley bus. c.1910. £8 - 10

An early 20th century photograph by the Aquarium. £18 - 20

CRESTED CHINA

The enthusiasm for crested miniatures can be attributed to the development of the railways in the second half of 19th century. Suddenly towns and coastal resorts became readily accessible to the Victorian/Edwardian public and throughout England the number of day-trippers and holidaymakers to these places grew yearly. Being within easy reach of London the Sussex seaside towns, from Bognor to Hastings, naturally reaped many benefits from the new found tourist trade who appeared willing to spend money on knick knacks.

By the 1880's, William Henry Goss, maker of fine heraldic china had spotted the possibility of a profitable niche for his business: the development of a range of china miniatures bearing the crest of the town of origin. This would be something for the visitor to take home as a souvenir and certainly something small enough to pop in a handbag or pocket.

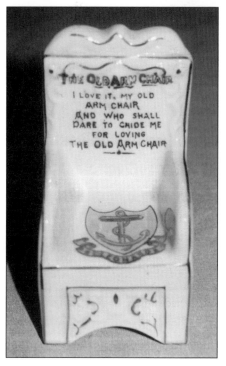

A crested Carlton china chair inscribed "The Old Arm Chair – I love it, my old arm chair: And who shall dare chide me for loving The Old Arm Chair". 3¹/₂ ins(9 cms) high. £22 - 25

His hunch proved correct. Goss crested china miniatures were fun, affordable and enormously popular. Animals, birds, buildings, figures, jugs, vases, novelty, militaria, furniture, transport, in fact almost anything could now be found in a tiny china look-a-like.

It was not long before other ceramic specialists had followed suit. These included Carlton, Arcadian, Grafton, Willow Art and Shelley. Yet although marginally cheaper their pieces were by no means as fine as those produced by the Goss factory and this is often reflected in the collectables market. However, today the subject is the really prime factor and whoever the maker, a rare example of a famous building will fetch more than a pretty cup and saucer, even if it has an unusual crest.

By the mid-1930's the production of crested china had stopped altogether. The craze for collecting these souvenirs, which had lasted overall for fifty years and peaked in Edwardian times, had died. Collections were discarded or gathered dust in the loft and it was not until the 1960's/70's that they resurfaced with the revival of interest in all Victoriana.

An Arcadian china Battle Abbey vase. 2 ins (5 cms) high. **£4 - 5**

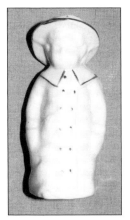

A Crowborough boy with the crest on his back. 3¹/₂ ins (9 cms) high. **£28 - 30**

A Foley china crested top hat inscribed 'Newhaven, Sussex'. 1¹/₂ ins (4 cms) high. **£12 - 14**

A crested Brighton wheelbarrow. 3 ins (7¹/₂ cms) long. **£10 - 12**

A Clifton china Brighton jug. **£4 - 5**

A St. Leonards crested china memorial. 5¹/₂ ins (14 cms) high. **£16 - 18**

An Arcadian china jug with the Crowborough crest. 2 ins (5 cms) high. **£7 - 8**

A Worthing jug , marked 'Exceller RBW'. 3 ins (7.5 cms) high. **£8 – 9**

An Arcadian Worthing vase. 2 ins (5cms) high. **£7 - 8**

Two pieces of Arcadian china with matching St. Leonards crests. Vase 3 ins (7.5 cms) high. **£6 - 7** Novelty teapot 2 ins (5 cms) high. **£15 - 17**

Three crested St. Leonards pots. From 2 ins (5 cms) to 3¹/₂ ins (9cms) high. **£6 – 8 each**

A Diamond china Bognor ewer. 2 ins (5 cms) high. **£6 - 7**

A crested Brighton cheese dish. 3 ins (7¹/₂ cms) long. **£11 - 13**

A Carlton ware Arundel pot 2¹/₂ ins (6.5 cms) high. **£4 - 5**

A Battle Abbey pot marked Cyclon. 3 ins (7.5 cms) high. **£10 - 12**

A crested Worthing two-handled vase. 2¹/₂ ins (6.5 cms) high. **£4 - 5**

An Arcadian china crested jug inscribed 'Henfield'. 3¹/₂ ins (9 cms) high. **£5 - 6**

A crested Grafton china bowl inscribed 'Littlehampton'. 2¹/₂ ins (6.5 cms) high. **£6 - 7**

A Swan china crested cap inscribed 'Eastbourne'. 2¹/₂ ins (6.5 cms) diameter **£20 - 24**

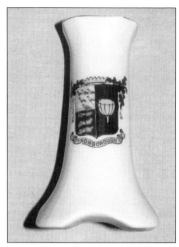

A crested Carlton china vase inscribed 'Crowborough'. 4 ins (10 cms) high. **£13 - 15**

A crested Bognor cat 4 ins (10 cms) high.
£25 - 30

A crested Hastings two-handled mug 1¹/₂ ins (4 cms) high. **£5 - 6**

A crested Lewes pot. 2 ins (5 cms) high. **£7 - 8**

An Arundel pot. 2 ins (5 cms) high. **£5 - 6**

A crested Hove dish and cover. 3¹/₂ ins (9 cms) diameter. **£9 - 10**

A crested Eastbourne teapot – minus the lid. 2¹/₂ ins (6.5 cms) high. **£11 - 12**

GLYNDEBOURNE OPERA

John Christie (1882 – 1962), best known as founder of the internationally famous Glyndebourne Festival Opera. But how did it begin? What led this man to build a theatre bang in the middle of the countryside? His interests were diverse too. Apart from opera he adored science, motor cars, gadgets of any sort and fine wines. His entrepreneurial character led him to invest (and not always wisely) in a number of business ventures. Partially blind with rounded features and balding by his middle years, he resembled an eccentric Pickwickian figure with an unconventional dress sense.

John was the only child of Augustus and Rosamond Christie, who were both locked in a loveless marriage primarily due to Augustus suffering frequent bouts of mental instability. Glyndebourne itself had passed into the Christie family during the first half of the 19th century. The original house was thought to date back to Tudor times but over the years constant extensions and alterations transformed it into a country mansion. By the time John was using Glyndebourne as his full time residence (his father preferring the family estates in Devon), he was referring, certainly to the Victorian Gothic additions, as "utterly hideous and something must be done".

The plans for the refurbishment began around 1916. By then, John was teaching science at his former school, Eton, having been invalided out of the Army. But as his passion for Glyndebourne grew, he decided to leave his post at Eton in 1922 to manage his estate full-time. He had a

A postcard of Glyndebourne. 1934 £2 - 3

strong sense of duty for the local community and by developing several companies to assist in the running of Glyndebourne created much needed employment within the area.

John's first major project at Glyndebourne was the building of an Organ Room, initially for his great friend, Dr. Charles Harford Lloyd, organist at the Chapel Royal in St. James. The story goes that Lloyd was about to retire and John suggested he move within the vicinity of Glyndebourne. "Only if there is a first class organ for me to play" he replied. Typically, John set about remedying the situation by constructing a room that was eighty feet in length and containing an organ of cathedral like proportions that took up the entire width.

The Organ Room eventually became the venue for concerts, recitals and operas and was almost certainly responsible for sowing the seeds in John's mind for a full scale theatre. There was also another contributory factor.

He had become a close friend of the Mounseys who, together with their four children, came to Glyndebourne as paying guests in 1923. Both were accomplished pianists, adored opera and included John in their many trips to Germany to indulge in the latest operatic performances. Fanny certainly was keen to be included in the musical development of Glyndebourne and proved to be something of a mentor to John. She also helped him to arrange the gatherings in the Organ Room, usually attended by friends, employees and local residents.

In December 1930, a travelling Opera Company came to Glyndebourne to give a performance. Amongst the cast was a young soprano, Audrey Mildmay. By the end of that evening, John Christie had fallen in love for the first - and last – time. In spite of Audrey's initial protests he courted her persistently and on 4th June 1931 they were married. Now with Audrey's creative expertise, Glyndebourne's place in operatic history was about to begin and almost simultaneously the foundations of the theatre were laid.

Three years later the first night of the Glyndebourne Opera Season took place with a flourish. It was on 28th May 1934 and on the day a special train brought guests in full evening dress from Victoria to Lewes, where the waiting coach took them on to Glyndebourne. For those who were setting eyes on Glyndebourne for the first time the scene must have held an almost fairy-tale quality; the wooded slopes of surrounding downland; the house, mellowed and tempered into classical lines by John's renovations; the gardens coloured with the flush of early summer. The Organ Room had been re-christened The Foyer and the theatre of simple design seated about three hundred. With Audrey playing Susanna in 'Figaro' on the first night ('Cosi Fan Tutte' on the second), the curtain rose

A postcard of the Opera House interior by Reeves, Lewes. 1937 £3 - 4

to an expectant audience. A few days later the season had sold out.

With fluctuating numbers, profits and losses, new ideas, more alterations, so the seasons came and went; each more frenetic as John strove for perfection. In spite of now having two children, Audrey still pursued her singing career but a recurring throat problem required essential rest.

The Second World War put a temporary halt on the regular opera festivities at Glyndebourne. John, overly concerned for his family, evacuated Audrey and the two children to Canada. They returned in 1944 and when Glyndebourne finally re-opened on 12th July 1946, it was to the World Premiere of Benjamin Britten's 'The Rape of Lucretia'. The following year 'Lucretia' was included once again as well as Britten's 'Albert Herring' and Gluck's 'Orpheus'. However the after effects of war, such as unemployment and rationing, put John in financial difficulties regarding his beloved opera.

In 1950 the Government offered a grant towards the production of four Mozart operas. Subsequently, the John Lewis Partnership, always loyal Glyndebourne supporters, stepped in with a further £12,500. The future looked brighter and in 1951, the Glyndebourne Season opened with Mozart's 'Idomeneo' followed by 'Figaro', 'Cosi Fan Tutte' and 'Don Giovanni'. Audrey had no part in these for once again she was seriously unwell. She never sang again and in May 1953 she died at the age of fifty-two.

A postcard of the Fly Tower and Green Room at Glyndebourne by Reeves, Lewes. £2 - 3

John was bereft. Although he still had Glyndebourne to occupy him, he was seventy-one and physically less able. Towards the end of the 1950's he handed over the Chairmanship of Glyndebourne to his son, George. John lived long enough to enjoy his first grandchild then, with his family around him, died peacefully at Glyndebourne on the 4th July 1962; fittingly as the performance of 'Cosi Fan Tutte' was about to begin.

Over the years the popularity of Glyndebourne Opera has remained undiminished. In 1987 this led George Christie to announce his plan of building a larger updated theatre to replace the old outgrown one. In true Christie fashion Glyndebourne was closed for as short a time as possible; after the season in 1992 and re-opening on 28th May 1994.

There's no doubt any Glyndebourne memorabilia has a magical quality to it. Each piece is evocative; a reminder of a scene or a voice or a summer's evening, for surely any collector will also be a lover of opera too. Here's a list of just a few things to look out for: - autographs, programmes, menus, theatre costume (rare) and accessories, books, records, postcards, posters, photographs and anything inscribed with Glyndebourne.

A Decca recording of Gluck's 'Orfeo ed Euridice' with Kathleen Ferrier, Glyndebourne Festival Chorus and the Southern Philharmonic Orchestra. Performed at Glyndebourne in 1947. £2 – 2.50p

'Where the Wild Things Are'. A fantasy from the London Sinfonietta conducted by Oliver Knussen. Glyndebourne Festival. c. 1980's. £1.50 – 2.50p

A recording of Mozart's 'Marriage of Figaro' by Glyndebourne Festival Productions conducted by Fritz Busch. 1934. £2 - 3

A Glyndebourne Festival Opera programme. 1963.
£5 - 6

A Glyndebourne Festival Opera programme. 1980.
£4 - 5

A Glyndebourne Festival Opera programme. 1981.
£5 - 6

Glyndebourne 2000. The season's programme.
£5 - 6

A postcard of John Brownlee as Don Giovanni from a drawing by Kenneth Green. *£1 - 2*

A postcard from a sketch of Glyndebourne. *1932. £1 - 2*

A postcard of Glyndebourne House and Opera with cattle grazing in foreground. *1935. £1.50 – 2*

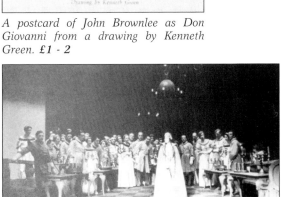

A postcard of 'Macbeth' at Glyndebourne 1934. *£2 – 2.50*

A postcard of another Glyndebourne production of 'Macbeth'. *1938 £1.50 - 2*

A postcard of the Witches Chorus, Macbeth, from a drawing by Kenneth Green. *1937. £1 - 2*

A second edition of the book entitled 'Shelley Memorials'. This was edited by Lady Shelley in 1859, with the added signature of Percy Bysshe Shelley. **£100 – 150.**

The Sussex County Cricket Club celebrate a hundred and fifty years with a commemorative plate 1839 – 1989. 10 ins (25.5 cms) diameter. **£25 - 35**

A Mottoware vase with a sailing boat and 'Eastbourne' written on the side. 4½ ins (11.5 cms) high. **£12 - 14**

A cup and saucer decorated with various views of Seaford. 5½ ins (13 cms) diameter, 3 ins (8cms) high. **£12 - 16**

A small mug illustrating the Pier at Bognor. 3 ins (7½ cms) high. **£4 – 5.**

A lidded heart shaped bowl decorated with flowers, a crest and 'Littlehampton' written below. 3½ ins (7.5 cms) long **£20 - 25**

A commemorative plate for the London Brighton & South Coast Railway to celebrate a hundred and fifty years in business. 1841 – 1991. **£12 - 15**

*A signed print of a downland scene with Firle Beacon in the background. The original was by Sussex artist, the late Frank Wootton and entitled 'Harvest Time'. 17¹/₂ ins x 27 ins (45 cms x 69 cms) **£80 – 120***

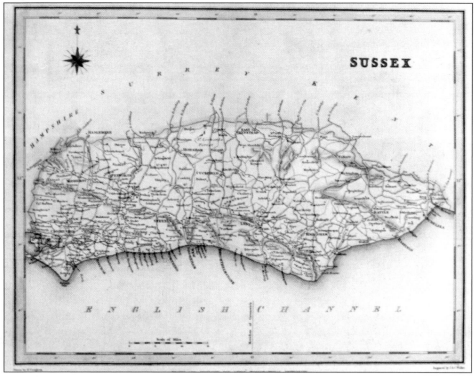

A framed map of Sussex taken from an old book c.1900. 7 ins x 9 ins (18cms x 23 cms).
£25 - 35

Eight 1980's badges illustrating various local businesses or services. **50p - £1 each.**

A selection of stoneware bottles from brewers, Albert Stone, Seaford; John Martin & Co., St. Leonards-on-Sea; King and Barnes Ltd., Horsham and L. Foord, Cross-in-Hand. Individual prices range from: - £35 (far left) to £150 (centre).

One of the few 'Green Top' ginger beer bottles sold by The Bognor & SC Mineral Water Company. 7½ ins (19 cms). £150 – 200.

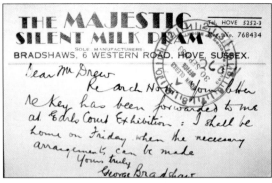

A postcard from The Majestic Silent Milk Pram situated in Western Road, Hove. 30th September 1938. *£2.50 – 3.00.*

An envelope with a collectable postmark from the Brighton Aquarium in 1892. *£4.50 – 5.50.*

A programme from the Imperial Theatre in North Street, Brighton, costing sixpence. *£4 – 4.50.*

1955 programme from the Brighton Sports Stadium advertising the Harlem Globetrotters. *£13 - 14*

1965. A programme from the Theatre Royal, Brighton. *£1 – 1.50.*

An Arcadian china crested Hove tortoise. 2$^{1}/_{2}$ ins. (6.5 cms) long. £30 – 35.

A crested Carlton china beaker inscribed 'Ye Olde Star Tune', Alfriston. 3 ins. (7$^{1}/_{2}$ cms) high. £12 – 14.

A Willow Art crested Brighton jug. 4 ins (10 cms) high. £7 - 8

Miniature jug bearing the crest of The Royal Sussex Regiment. £20 - 25.

The HMS Hampshire, the Peruvian and the Sussex cliffs, the Seven Sisters, were painted on ivory nuts by an unknown Sussex sailor around the beginning of the 20th century. £45 - 65 each.

The brass bell from Brighton V, launched in 1932 as a passenger ship. Subsequently, she was used as a wartime troopship before being bombed in Dieppe Harbour in 1940. 13 ins (33 cms) high. £300 – 400.

Parker Duofolds (left to right), Junior Red c.1924. £150 – 200. Lady Green jade pencil c.1927. £60 – 80. Lady Mandarin yellow c. 1928. £150 – 250. Junior Red pencil c.1927. £50 – 90. Streamlined Duofold special lapis blue c.1929. £200 – 300. Senior de luxe Moderne pearl and black c.1932. £600 – 700. Senior de luxe Moderne green pearl pencil c.1930. £90 – 130. Junior burgundy and black pen c.1930. £80 – 120. Junior jade green pen c.1929. £150 – 200. Junior de luxe Moderne green and pearl pencil c.1929. £60 – 80. Junior de luxe Moderne green/pearl and black pen c.1932. £80 – 120. (Horizontal) Lucky Curve Senior Duofold pen in mandarin yellow c.1927. £200 – 250.

Nine rare and almost priceless examples of early Parker pens in mint condition. A gold filigree Snake pen (3rd from right) sold at auction in 1994 for £14,500. (From left to right) No 43 gold filled c.1908. No.16 gold filled filigree over red hard rubber c.1903. No.15 gold filled over black hard rubber serrated pearl and abalone sides c.1906. No.28 bakelite barrel Demonstrator c.1916. Giant red hard rubber sterling silver band c.1909. No.10 'Twist' red and black hard rubber c.1905. No.38 'Snake' gold filled filigree over black hard rubber, green stone snake eyes c.1906. No.47 gold filled cap, pearl sided barrel c.1905. No.20 red and black mottled hard rubber, turban safety cap c.1912.

JUDGES' POSTCARDS

The stretch of road known as 'Judges Bend' appears little different to any other part of the coastal thoroughfare between Bexhill and Hastings. Yet amongst the confusion of traffic and buildings, an Art Deco structure with the distinct undertones of a continental villa, faces the sea. This is the home of Judges' Postcards, virtually unchanged since it was built in 1927 by its founder, Fred Judge.

Fred Judge was born in Wakefield, Yorkshire in 1872, just two years after the first British postcard had been issued by the G.P.O. Complete with a printed stamp, these were designed to take the address on one side and the message together with a small illustration on the other. As yet this was of

Judges' Postcards. St. Leonards-on-Sea £3 - 4

little interest to Judge who, eventually on leaving school, began work as an engineer; photography was simply a hobby.

In pursuit of this interest he took a holiday in Sussex and whilst exploring, discovered and fell in love with Hastings. That was in 1901. Within a year Fred Judge had left Wakefield and engineering behind and, joined by his brother Thomas, bought a photographic shop at 21a Wellington Place, Hastings. Coincidentally, at the same time, an Act of Parliament allowed the message and the address to be written on one side of a postcard leaving the other free for a picture. This was to be the ideal vehicle for Judge's artistic ability and by 1903 his photographic postcards capturing local scenes were being sold at Judges' Photo Stores.

On the 6th June 1904, the violent storm that lit up the night sky above Hastings can directly be attributed to the beginning of Judge's success story. On that night Judge was out with his camera anxious to capture the visual effects of such a storm. The result was a unique arch of lightning from East to West, with an ominously darkened foreground of fishing boats. Over 25,000 copies of 'Lightning' were sold in one year and it remained a best seller for over a quarter of a century.

Two years later, 'Glory', a view of Hastings Old Town and Parish Church from East Hill was published. This is thought to be Judge's finest postcard and illustrates his mastery with the camera together with his ability to catch the depths of light and shade of any scene.

As the business grew, so did the necessity for bigger and better

The famous postcard 'Lightning'. 1904. **£1 – 1.50p**   *'Glory'. 1906.* **80p - £1.25p**

premises. After several moves, this finally culminated in 1927 with Judges' present purpose built site at Bexhill Road, St. Leonards-on-Sea. By this date branches in London, the West Country and the Lake District had been opened and the range of places featured on postcards extended.

In 1950, at the age of 78, Fred Judge died. As he'd requested his ashes, accompanied by the cry of seagulls, were scattered on East Hill, Hastings, near to the spot where he'd taken 'Glory' many years earlier.

Throughout his career Judge exhibited many of his pictures worldwide. Their strongly impressionistic nature won him over a hundred medals and international respect as both a photographer and canny businessman. His death, however, did not spell the end of Judges' Postcards. Instead it was bought by fellow photographer, Ernest Bartholomew, who expanded the business and introduced lithographic colour printing.

On Bartholomew's retirement in 1984, Judges' Postcards was taken over by Bernard and Jan Wolford, both of whom had a wealth of experience in industry, management and factory organisation. Today, they have been joined by their two sons and with Graeme as Managing Director and Trevor as Sales Director, the family will continue to build on the foundations laid out by Fred Judge at the beginning of the 20th century.

Rough sea at Hastings. £1 - 2

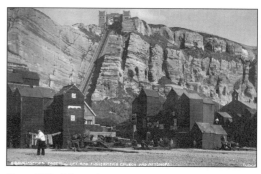

East Hill lift and Fisherman's Church and Net Shops. £2 - 3

Hastings. £1 -2

Hastings and the Pier. 80p - £1.20

De la Warr Pavilion. Bexhill-on-Sea. £1 – 1.25p

Mermaid Street, Rye. £1 – 1.25p

Beachy Head and Belle Tout Lighthouse. 80p - £1.20.

The Old Windmill, Alfriston. £1.50 - £2.00.

Clayton Mills, near Brighton. £2 – 2.50p

West Blatchington Mill, near Brighton. £2 - 3

Ploughing on the Downs at Kemp Town. £2 - 3

On the beach at Brighton. £2.50p - £3

The beach, Kemp Town, Brighton. £3.50p - £4.50p

Boating Pool, Brighton. £2.50p - £3

The White Horse, Hindover Hill, near Seaford.
£1.00 - £1.25.

The Meanders of the River Cuckmere.
£1.00 - £1.50.

High Street, Alfriston. £1.50 - £2

The Market Cross, Alfriston. £1.50 - £2

The Seven Sisters from Seaford Head. 50p - £1

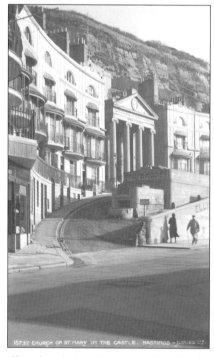

Church of St. Mary in the Castle, Hastings. £1 – 1.25p

The Lobster Man. Eastbourne. £1 - 1.50p

MARITIME

It takes little to realise the nautical scenery of Sussex is as much a part of the landscape as the South Downs. That restless stretch of the English Channel dividing our coastline from France and the rest of Europe has ensured centuries of history rich in seafaring trade. This, of course, has provided an unending source of salty memorabilia for both dealers and collectors to bargain with on dry land.

Throughout the last two thousand years the towns of Rye, Winchelsea, Hastings, Pevensey, Seaford, Newhaven, Lewes, Brighton, Shoreham, Arundel, Littlehampton and Chichester have, at some point, played a varying role of maritime importance. This was dictated by evolution, coastal erosion and the fluctuating fortunes of progress – or war. After all, the Battle of Hastings, undoubtedly the most famous invasion, took place in Sussex when William the Conqueror landed at Pevensey in 1066.

Since then great ships have been built at Rye, cargoes of spices and wine have been unloaded at Shoreham, fish have been caught at Hastings and Sussex wool has been exported, either legally or illegally, from all sorts of places. And then, with the introduction of the 19th century pleasure boats and cross-channel steamers, a new industry presented itself as the Victorians indulged in the delights of sea travel. By this time the only ports of any significance were Rye, Newhaven, Shoreham, Littlehampton and Chichester, although the latter declined sharply after the opening of the Brighton – Portsmouth railway line in the 1840's.

Rye's road to affluence began in the 15th century when it replaced the neighbouring port of Winchelsea, which was literally left high and dry as the sea slowly receded. For two hundred years Rye commanded one of the best harbours in the south-east and could provide shelter for more than four hundred ships until, like its predecessor, that too began to silt up. However, constant clearing of the shifting sand and shingle ensured the continuation of the boat building and the fishing industries, but the days as a major port were numbered. One by one the wealthy merchants departed.

Even so, the records of the 1850's indicate the port still owned about fifty ships and at least half a dozen had been built there in one year alone. Names like Marion Zagury, Anderida, Effort, Topsy and Lord Dacre have the essence of a Cornish novel; in reality the boats were all launched from Rye. Now those old timber warehouses on Strand Quay are filled with antique shops and collectors search amongst the 'old' and 'not so old' pieces for a seafaring relic.

Thirty miles west of Rye at the mouth of the River Ouse is Newhaven, a Victorian harbour that once rated, in terms of revenue, as the sixth most important in England. Today, the constant to-ing and fro-ing of cross-channel steamers, the hustle and bustle of passengers or the noise of cargoes being loaded, is a thing of the past.

Newhaven's commercial dalliance began in earnest when the London, Brighton and South Coast Railway provided a rail link to Newhaven in 1847. The company also invested heavily in the port itself and ordered three new paddle steamers, Brighton, Newhaven and Dieppe. These three boats made regular crossings to Dieppe which took over from the twice weekly service that had been in operation since 1825. In those days the journey took nine hours. Within forty years the duration had been halved.

Events such as the Paris Exhibition of 1878 caused a flurry amongst the

Small unmarked mug showing a picture of Newhaven harbour and the words - 'The Ferry, Newhaven'. 2¹/₂ ins (6 cms) high. £25 - 35.

port investors who, on this particular occasion, ordered two more steamers, another Brighton and Victoria to accommodate the extra passengers. Unfortunately, neither of these vessels were destined to have long lives. In 1887 Victoria struck rocks off the coast of Pointe d'Ailly and sank with the loss of several lives. Seven years later, Brighton also sank, this time in Dieppe harbour after hitting a pier.

As the fortunes of Newhaven's steamers waxed and waned, ships such as Brighton, Orleans, Paris, Sussex, Rouen and Brittany were replaced by updated namesakes. Some were used as troop ships in the World Wars. The 1960's saw perhaps the last of the charismatic ferries, Villandry and Valencay; then in 1973 Sealink's spanking new 5000 ton ship came into service. Almost inevitably, that too has become history and the archives have joined those of other Sussex ships in Newhaven's Maritime Museum.

c. 1880. Unmarked blue and white jug with the emblem of the Newhaven and Dieppe Steam Packets. 7 ins (17.5 cms) high. £90 - 110.

In contrast, Shoreham never developed as a cross-channel port largely due to the inability of the London, Brighton and South Coast Railway reaching an agreement with the port authorities. Instead, the trade came from the shipbuilding that flourished in the Victorian era. A number of the great ships that voyaged round the world were constructed by Shoreham based companies such as James Britton Balley, May and Thwaites, John Shuttleworth and Dyer & Son. At one point, the port owned more than a hundred and fifty barques and brigs with at least half of them being locally built. By the time the twentieth century dawned, Shoreham's commercial interests had altered. Apart from small craft, shipbuilding had largely ceased with the introduction of metal vessels. Instead, as it had done in medieval times, the port concentrated on handling the increasing amount of freight. New wharves, derricks and storage tanks were created in order to handle oil, coal, timber and agricultural produce. In the late 1950's a large wine terminal was built to accommodate quantities of Spanish sherry. Today, the seemingly ongoing work on the area of the new harbour has made Shoreham one of the main ports on the South Coast.

Quayside Littlehampton, whose extended boundaries have virtually merged into the urban sprawl of Rustington and Worthing, still retains an ancient seafaring charm. It lies on the River Arun and, unlike Newhaven, only benefited briefly from the Railway Company's investment in cross-channel ferries. From 1863, when the branch line to the port opened, picture postcard steamers took passengers to Honfleur, Caen, St Malo and the Channel Islands. Following the same route cargo boats imported Jersey potatoes, wine, brandy and fruit, whilst our exports consisted mainly of manufactured goods.

As the ferry service flourished, so the 19th century Arun shipyards continued to prosper; their ships visiting the romantic shores of India, South Africa, America and the Falklands. Then the rapid decline in wooden built hulls began, which also coincided with the Railway Company withdrawing their cross-channel steamers in 1883. For some years the building of small craft survived, but Littlehampton's golden era had passed and, sadly, the town never regained its former importance as a harbour. Now small boats fill the modern marinas and the bric-a-

c. 1880. Willow covered fresh water bottle used in the old rowing boats' lifeboats. £100 - 130

brac that clutters the intermittent antique shops holds a certain nautical promise.

This brief outline on some of the Sussex ports is mainly for landlubbers and would-be collectors to illustrate a mere fraction of the possibilities for ocean-going memorabilia. Local museums offer a wealth of information on maritime Sussex and libraries have a number of books on the subject. After that it's down to scouring the Auctions, Antique Fairs, Boot Fairs and shops for a bargain. And don't forget to look for the barnacle-encrusted goodies that may have found their way to the surface from the shipwrecks that litter the Channel: or from the lifeboats that went to their rescue.

There could even be scope for a collection based on the Hastings fishing fleet, once the largest in Europe and whose tarred net shops still stand like blackened sentinels guarding decades of seafaring history.

1896. Water colour of 'Peruvian' by the French artist, Eugene Grandin. Newhaven Museum.

Modern 'Ship in the Bottle' model of the HMS Brazen.
£30- 40

Wooden sand fire bucket from Brighton VI. **£55 - 65**

Homemade Dancing Dolls were occasionally used by sailors or fishermen to earn extra money. The doll was held by a handle at the back and 'jigged' up and down so as the hands and feet make a loud tap-dancing noise to accompanying music.

A sailor's Dancing Doll (some damage) Approx. 14 ins (36 cms) high. **£80 - 100**

Unmarked cup and saucer bearing the crest of an anchor and the words 'Newhaven, Sussex 1894'. **£18 - 25**

c. 1880. Brass ship's gimbal candle lamp, found hanging in a derelict cabin on a Sussex wharf. 12 ins (31 cms) high. **£100 -120**

Brass capstan cover from the 'Peruvian', shipwrecked in Seaford Bay in 1899. 18 ins (46 cms) diameter. **£400 - 500**

c. 1887. Egg cup – Newhaven to Dieppe Steam Packet. 1¹/₂ ins (4.5 cms) high. **£22 - 24**

Crested Shelley jug with the words 'Newhaven, Sussex'. C. 1910 2¹/₂ ins (6 cms) high. **£20 - 25**

c. 1970. Small dish inscribed with the words 'Big Fleet' and 'Dunkerque – Calais – Dieppe SNCF Dover – Folkestone – Newhaven. 4¹/₂ ins (11.5 cms) diameter. **£8 - 10**

Atkins patent Water Softener. This particular piece was used in the Saloon Bar of The London & Paris Hotel, which was built in the mid-19th century on the quayside at Newhaven. 16 ins (40.5 cms) high **£100 - 140**

Coloured bloater paste pot with some chips to the rim. 4¹/₂ ins (11.5 cms) high. **£35 - 45**

A photograph of the Bordeaux (1864 – 90) berthed outside the London & Paris Hotel, Newhaven. **£6 – 7.**

A Postcard of the cross-channel steamer nearing Dieppe. c. 1908. **£4 – 6.**

A postcard of the cross-channel steamer leaving Newhaven. **£4 – 6.**

PARKER PENS

Even today the merest whisper of a Parker 51 will send a frisson of delight down the spine of pen enthusiasts. Thought by many to be the grandfather of all writing instruments, the Parker 51 was launched in 1941 to commemorate Parker Pen's 51st anniversary. It also coincided with their buy-out of the Valentine Pen Company, whose premises were situated at Newhaven Harbour in East Sussex. In spite of the fact that Parker had owned offices in London since the beginning of the 20th century, Newhaven provided their first UK production centre. By then Parker, whose success story started some fifty years earlier in America, was known as the largest pen manufacturer in the world. Almost every pen design became the forerunner of a complete range, constantly updated and made in several colours or finishes, all of which adds to their individuality and current rarity value.

Undoubtedly, Parker Pens can attribute their snowball success to one man's unshakable belief in his invention of the ultimate pen. That man was George Parker, teacher and part time salesman for the John Holland Fountain Pen Company who, in the unlikely setting of a back street hotel bedroom in

An early 1950's Parker 51. One of its notable features was the 'hooded' nib. **£90 - 120**

Janesville, Wisconsin, wrestled with the complexities of designing the perfect pen. Already well versed in the art of pen repairs, he was looking to create a pen that eliminated the infrequent supply of ink to the nib which alternatively caused scratchy writing, blotches and inky fingers. On 10th December 1889, George Parker had his first design patented. More followed and within two years an acquaintance of Parker's, insurance salesman, W. F. Palmer, had bought himself a half share in an unknown pen business. His cheque was made out to The Parker Pen Company.

In 1894, George Parker introduced a revolutionary new pen, the Lucky Curve. The capillary type action of this pen, the first of its kind, promised to put an end to ink stains and blotches. Judging by its huge popularity the Lucky Curve must have lived up to all those promises, for it was improved and modified over the next ten years and eventually enabled the Parker Pen Company to move to larger premises in Janesville. By the end of the 19th century, George Parker had nearly 9000 dealers in the United States

An advertisement from the Penny Pictorial Magazine. c.1895.

selling his pens, which must have created considerable sales, yet it's rare to find a pre-1900 Parker and the few examples that remain sell to collectors for very high prices.

By 1908, with overseas distribution rapidly expanding, Parker was reported to be the most prolific international pen company. His pens were not just utilitarian objects; they had become both fashion and status symbols. With this in mind, Parker created his most opulent range of writing instruments so far, by using the combination of gold, silver and mother-of-pearl overlays. Amongst these was the extravagant Snake Pen which depicted gold or silver snakes with glinting green eyes entwined around the barrel. Today it's reckoned there are only about fifty original snake pens in existence so it's not surprising that when one came up for auction at Bonham's in 1994, it fetched £14,500. Interestingly, three years earlier, when Parker had sponsored a pen auction in Geneva, Switzerland, the same Snake Pen sold for a mere £11,000. In 1998 Parker released a limited edition and updated version of the Snake Pen.

The launching of the Duofold in 1921 proved to be one of the company's most celebrated pens and still remains a favourite amongst vintage pen collectors. Sporting a gold nib that was guaranteed to write for twenty-five years, the Duofold was twice as expensive as the average pen. This made many doubt its saleability. Fortunately, George Parker's two sons had followed him into the business and the younger, Kenneth, a firm believer in advertising, masterminded an ingenious marketing strategy for the Duofold. His belief paid off as sales soared to a new zenith. Sir Arthur Conan Doyle, of Sherlock Holmes fame, was quoted as saying, "I have, at last, met my affinity in pens." The Duofold was eventually replaced in popularity by the Vacumatic in 1933; a design initially presenting a 'see-through' laminated barrel in narrow stripes of black and pearl.

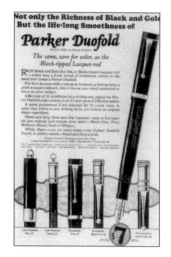

Little changed at Parker Pens when George Parker died in 1937. His sons, (as would his grandsons,) ensured all their father's traditions, beliefs and mark of quality would continue in this essentially family run business.

c. 1934. Vacumatic Oversize pen with laminated pearl barrel. £150 - 200.

In 1941 the introduction of the famous Parker 51 was promoted as being 'like a pen from another world'. It also commemorated Parker's 51st anniversary and coincided with the acquisition of their UK factory at Newhaven. Initially, production at Newhaven had to be geared to making wartime weapon components and only 20% of the output was devoted to pens, many of which were supplied to the Forces. With Parker already having a reputation for their pens being used in historic signings, it seemed only fitting that a Parker 51 was used to sign the agreement ending World War II on the European front. On this occasion the pen belonged to General Dwight D. Eisenhower. In 1950 the legendary 51 went on to receive the Fashion Academy Award for Styling, Precision and Craftsmanship.

The years that followed the war heralded times of great change and Parker Pen adapted accordingly. A much cheaper pen, the Parker 21, captured the lower end of the market; superchrome permanent ink was available in five colours; the first ballpoint pen by Parker, the Jotter with a T-Ball tip was released in 1954, followed by the Liquid Lead Pencil. The classic Parker 61 was issued in 1956 and the Parker 45 with an ink cartridge in 1960. In 1962, Parker Pens were awarded the Royal Warrant as sole suppliers of pens and ink to the Royal Household, and in the mid-1960's a Special Edition pen was made from parts of the first American space rocket to carry an astronaut into space.

The handsome Parker 75, made of solid sterling silver trimmed with gold, was announced in 1964 and due to its enormous success the range was extended within a year. In 1970, the Parker TI was made almost entirely from titanium and dubbed as the world's toughest pen – in fact the metal was so tough, it proved too hard to manufacture and production was discontinued a year later. This of course makes the TI highly desirable and gives it a sale price of around £300 - 400.

During the 1960's and 1970's Parker released several Limited Edition Specials using the Parker 75. Amongst these was the Spanish Treasure Fleet Edition – crafted from the silver salvaged from Spanish treasure ships sunk off the coast of Florida in 1715: a pewter American Bicentennial pen with a relic from Independence Hall, Philadelphia, in the cap and the much coveted RMS Queen Elizabeth Edition, fashioned out of the brass retrieved from the liner which sank in Hong Kong harbour in 1972.

The first Parker Fibre Tip pen was introduced to the UK in 1971. The Rollerball pen appeared in 1975 and the UK version followed six years later. The Slinger in 1976 became known as 'the pen you wear'. In 1981 the Arrow range was announced and then in 1983 came Parker's most luxurious range of pens to date, the Premier Collection, created from gold, sterling silver or chinese laque.

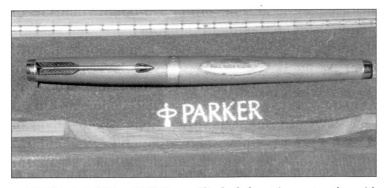

c. 1974 Limited Edition RMS Queen Elizabeth fountain pen together with box and certificate of authenticity. £500 - 700.

Apart from the 1980's preceding Parker Pen's centenary, it also introduced a wind of change. In 1986 a management buy-out took place resulting in the worldwide writing instrument rights being transferred to Newhaven. But little altered and the production of new designs continued unabated as the founder's philosophy of innovation and quality remained firmly in place. An updated version of the legendary 1920's Duofold was re-introduced to mark the company's 100th anniversary. Then in 1993 Parker Pens was sold yet again; this time to Gillette Stationery Products, alongside Waterman, Liquid Paper and PaperMate.

It would be impossible in this brief summary of The Parker Pen Company to catalogue all the pens they've produced in the last hundred years. But if these few pages fan an interest in Parker's past writing instruments, there are two important factors to bear in mind if starting to collect. Firstly, condition is paramount and affects the value enormously. And secondly, age is not necessarily the most desirable; rarity is far more important and even unusual ball pens will fetch a good price.

Meanwhile, as Parker Pens moves into the 21st century, the company is under the new ownership of Newell Rubbermaid, within their stationery division, Sanford. This is now the largest stationery company in the world, owning numerous brand names which include Sharpie, Rotring, Reynolds, Waterman, PaperMate and, of course, Parker. The site at Newhaven will remain the European Headquarters for Sanford and, with new ranges under wraps, Parker will undoubtedly continue to find their pens of today become tomorrow's memorabilia.

A selection of Parker pens in fair condition. From the top downwards: -

A green Parker '17'. c. 1964.	**£38 – 45**
A Parker '61' c. 1956.	**£40 – 55**
A blue Parker 'Rialto'. c. 1994.	**£30 - 35**
A rolled gold Parker '45' c. 1964	**£40 - 55**

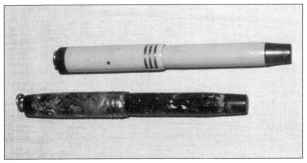

Two Duofold ladies pens with a ring at the top of the cap for wearing on a chain. £140 – 180 each.

Three examples of Parker Duofolds. Left to right: Black c.1924, £80 - 120; Red c.1927, £150 - 200; Lapis Blue.1929, £200 – 250.

The Vacumatic pen, introduced in 1933, had three distinct features: a revolutionary filling system that employed vacuum pressure; a laminated pearl barrel and a new Arrow pocket clip. This became Parker's trademark.

The same Vacumatic was also made in a number of unusual variations including the Holy Water Sprinkler, which didn't actually write. This particular 'pen' was semi-transparent so the priest could see, in church, how much Holy Water remained in the barrel.

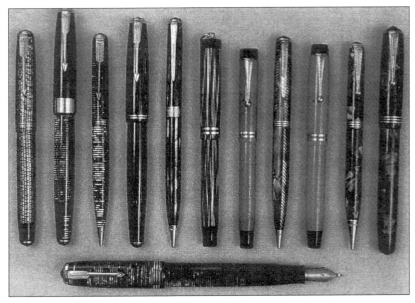

Parker Vacumatic and Duofold pens and pencils in mint condition.
Left to right: Junior golden web c. 1936; Major emerald pearl solid 9 ct gold band c. 1939; Standard silver pearl c. 1934; Junior green shadow wave 1939; Pink, silver and black c. 1941; True blue 1928; Pastel moiré magenta 1928; Royal Challenger brown herringbone and brown marble c. 1938; Pastel moiré coral c. 1932; De Luxe Challenger, gold and black marble c. 1937; Burgundy and black marble c. 1937. From £100 – 250 each.

Horizontal: Oversize Vacumatic burgundy pearl c. 1934 £150 - 200.

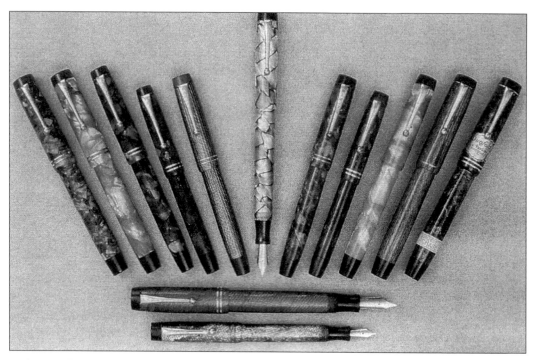

Parker Duofold and Victory pens c. 1935 – 44, in mint condition. Left to right: Senior light and dark brown pearl; Senior light and dark gold pearl; Special burgundy pearl and black marble; Juniorette (Lady) turquoise (blue and gold); Junior green and black lizard; Victory black lined pearl;; Junior light and dark burgundy pearl; Juniorette green and bronze marble; Victory gold and yellow pearl; Senior brown and black lizard; Senior light and dark blue pearl. Horizontal: Top; Senior rose and black lizard. Bottom; Juniorette silver and black lizard. From **£120 – 300** *each. N.B. The Lizard examples of the pens shown above often fetch a much higher price depending on rarity and condition.*

An original Valentine pen c. 1940 **£80 – 100.**

Three late 1940's Parker 51 pens, all in rare colours. Left to right: Mustard, Forest Green and Cocoa. **£90 - 150 each.**

Black 1940's Parker Pen displaying the 'button filler'. **£95 – 120.**

Parker Arrow black GT pen and Ballpen. £50 – 80.(2).

A 1960's Parker ruby glass desk base with black tapered pen. £125 - 175.

Parker 75 Sterling Silver Pen and Ballpen. 1980's £80 – 120.(2).

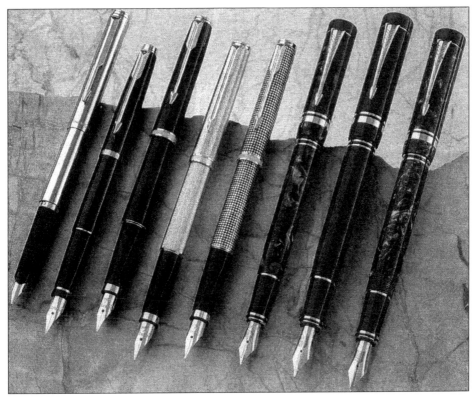

A selection of modern fountain pens from Parker's International range in the 1990's in mint condition. £80 – 200 each.

Rodmell Pottery 1954 – 62. Oval terracotta dish glazed with blue flowers on a white background. 16 ins (41 cms) long. £25 – 30.

Hastings Pottery c.1956 – 95. A mushroom-shaped bowl marked 'Denis Lucas'. £10 – 12.

A treacle glazed studio vase by Ray Everett. 12 ins (30.5 cms) high. £40 – 50.

An Iden Pottery jug 4½ ins (11.5 cms) high. £10 – 12.

Two small pots by Ray Everett. £12 – 18 each.

c.1925. An unusual Dicker bowl in a blue and brown cold glaze.
6 ins (15.5 cms) diameter. **£65 – 75.**

Green and brown glazed Dicker jug
bearing the inscription, "Come
brothers shall we joyn – give me your
two pennies". c.1920's. 7 ins (18 cms)
high. **£140 – 160.**

c.1920. Dicker vase in iron lustre glaze. 10½
ins (27 cms) high. **£50 – 60.**

A Dicker treacle ware jug with a glazed green interior.
9½ ins (24 cms) high. **£75 – 100.**

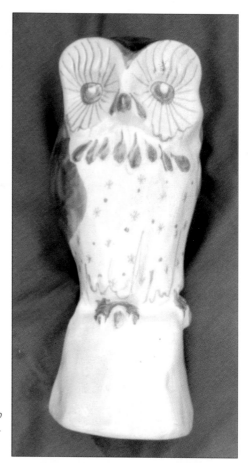

An unusual David Sharp mud-glazed pottery money-box in the form of a gorilla. Late 1970's. 7¹/₂ ins (19 cms) high. £50 - 60.

c. 1970's. A David Sharp green/blue floral patterned owl. 11 ins (28 cms) high. £45 – 55.

A 1970's David Sharp mottled pottery duck in the form of a money box. 12 ins (30 cms) long. £40 – 50.

A 1950's multi-coloured Rye Pottery vase by David Sharp. 13 ins (33 cms) high. In the collection of Rye Pottery.

A Rye Pottery cockerel vase c.1955. 6¹/₂ ins (16.5 cms) high. £140 – 160.

Two decorative 1970's Rye Pottery plates. 4 ins (10 cms) and 5 ins (13 cms) diameter. £20 – 25.

c.1980's. A striped Rye Pottery lamp. 6¹/₂ ins (16.5 cms) high. £50 - 60

A Sussex tip cart, used in the 19th/20th centuries for potatoes, manure etc. £600 – 800.

A blue painted iron foot plough c.1900 £55 – 65.

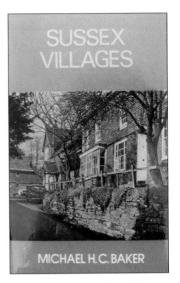

'View of Sussex' by Ben Darby and published by Robert Hale & Co. 1975 **£6 – 7.**

'Sussex' by John Burke, published by B.T.Batsford. 1974. **£6 – 7.**

'Sussex Villages' by Michael H.C. Baker, published by Robert Hale. 1977. **£6 – 7.**

1983. A watercolour by Elizabeth Bury from the book 'Glyndebourne – The Gardens' written by Anne Scott-James and Christopher Lloyd. **£3 – 4.**

Officer's full dress helmet. c1920. The Royal Sussex Regiment. £350 – 400.

19th century Sussex grate. Also known as a Duck's Nest Grate, this smaller design probably coincided with the introduction of coal. 24 ins (61 cms) wide. **£250 – 300.**

A pair of 18th century decorative Wealden firedogs. 33 ins (84 cms) high. **£245 – 295.**

17th c. iron trug or garden basket. 18 ins (45.5 cms) long. **£100 – 125.**

A cast iron fireback from the former Phoenix Ironworks in Lewes. **£265 – 295.**

18th century firedogs or andirons supporting a log basket. **£250 – 300.**

POTTERY

Although pottery has been made in Sussex since medieval times, the characteristic brown ware appeared mainly in evidence from the late 18th century onwards. This rich red pottery, caused by an excess of iron in the clay which sometimes gave it a curious flecked appearance, was highly glazed and often decorated with cream motifs, stars or inscriptions.

During the first half of the 19th century there were over thirty working pottery sites in this county alone. But bearing in mind potteries were often simply a family business, supplying only their local community with all forms of pottery including bricks and tiles, this number is hardly surprising.

In the past it was a relatively easy matter to become a potter whose trades, out of financial necessity, were usually diverse. All that was required was a licence to dig on an appropriate piece of land containing the right type of clay, sufficient timber to fire the kiln and a nearby stream. Having agreed a rental with the landowner the potter was in business. However, the process of achieving workable clay was far more involved.

Initially the clay had to be dug from the ground, preferably in the autumn. It was then left to be 'broken down' by the frosts for a few months before being combined with water and shovelled into a pug mill to be thoroughly mixed. Afterwards, it would be layered between old sacking until ready for use, when chunks would be broken off and grit and stones removed before being rolled into balls. At last the clay was ready for the potter to throw his pots which, when done, were left to dry out before additions such as handles, glazing and slip decorations were applied; slip is the name given to clay diluted with water to form a creamy liquid used in the ornamentation of earthenware vessels. Next, the pottery had to be carefully placed in the kiln, which usually reached a temperature of around 1000 C. After firing had taken place, the fires were put out and the wares left to cool in the kiln for several days.

Such was the process for the potter until the end of the 19th century when potteries in the Midlands made use of modern methods to produce cheaper, lighter wares in greater quantity. This coincided with Sussex clay becoming scarcer and restrictions being imposed by the Board of Trade on the hitherto effective and cheap but highly poisonous lead glaze used by local potters.

The following gazetteer of principle Sussex potteries covers only those which survived the intrusion of mass production and continued in business until well into the 20th century. More recently – say in the last fifty years – a number of new potteries have been established throughout Sussex. Some have had a brief life, others have found ongoing success by selling an innovative range of household pottery, plaques, vases, chargers and animals as well as those much sought after, one off studio pieces.

Burgess Hill Situated in the area that was once called St. John's Common, the Burgess Hill pottery was actually a sprawling combination of four potteries, initially run by four families. Generally, all four produced items in brown ware as well as bricks and tiles. These four sites appear to have been established at different times during the first half of the 19th century and apart from one, had closed by 1920. The remaining site which had been run by the Meeds family since 1850, made a variety of glazed and unglazed flower, seakale and rhubarb pots, pitchers, jars, household crockery, miniature pieces, sparrow and mole traps.

Burgess Hill continued to produce pottery until 1941, when it finally closed due to the wartime blackout restrictions.

Chailey Originally two rival potteries existed at Chailey, one owned by the Alcorns, the other by the Normans. Both produced more or less identical items in brown ware with inlaid decorations or a verse such as this one inscribed on a tobacco canister made for John Oden in 1839: -

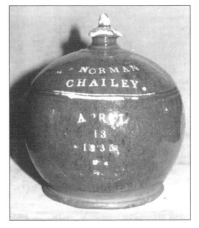

A turnip shaped brown ware money box from the Chailey Pottery inscribed 'Ann Norman, Chailey. April 13, 1835'. Anne of Cleves House Museum.

My tobacco I do put
Within this little pot
And my friend may have a pipe
If any I have got.

Ditties like these, names and dates were incorporated on flower pots, urns, punch bowls, flasks, money boxes, mugs and jars.

In the late 19th century, the Alcorns were bought out by the Normans, whose pottery skills encompassed the entire family and continued down the line until the death of the sixth Richard Norman in 1930. During this era some of the pieces had an impressed mark on the base with the name E & R Norman, Chailey Potteries, near Lewes, Sussex. From 1930 onwards Richard's partner, Wallace William, took over as sole owner supplying the London store, Heals, with traditional brown ware until the pottery closed in 1939.

Dicker The date the first pottery opened at Dicker, near Hailsham, is uncertain, but a notice in the Sussex Weekly Advertiser of December 1774, records the acrimonious demise of the partnership between potters, Thomas Wood and William Cuckney. As each set about establishing an individual pottery, their petty squabbling continued by means of a series of notices being placed in the newspaper. These, in essence, assured customers of the best attention and then requested them to disregard any malicious statements given by their rival.

Nevertheless, by 1776, Thomas Wood was bankrupt and his business sold to a Thomas and James Peckham.

Until the end of the 19th century the history of these two potteries is rather nebulous, although records indicate the Dicker Pottery was acquired by Uriah Clark in 1845.

When its competitor, the Boship Pottery, closed in the

A Dicker earthenware loving cup probably by Benjamin William Henry Bridges, marked UC&N on the underside. c.1912. 3¹/₂ ins (9 cms) high. £75 - 85

1890's the potter, Benjamin William Henry Bridges literally crossed the road and joined Uriah Clark at Dicker. Benjamin's speciality was reproducing old Sussex slipware including the design and date. Although these rather rare pieces are collectable in their own right, they should not be confused with the value of the originals.

When Uriah Clark took over the Dicker Pottery he was a young man, and one of many talents. In directories, from the 1850's onwards, he's variously listed as a brown ware potter, grocer, draper, blacksmith, coal and coke merchant and brick manufacturer. Apparently reasonably wealthy he died in 1903 and in 1912 the pottery was officially established as Uriah Clark and Nephew; the mark being U C & N, Dicker, Sussex, or old Sussex Ware.

A Dicker iron lustre jug 4 ins (10 cms) high. £25 - 35

By the 1920's the Dicker Pottery had grown apace and become a thriving commercial enterprise. Now there were twenty or more employees producing over two hundred examples of pottery in assorted shapes, sizes and glazes. Publicity material suggested visitors to Sussex should take a drive into the country and see pottery in its different stages of production at the Dicker factory.

A distinguishing and popular feature of some Dicker ware were those pieces finished in the rich black iron lustre glaze: coloured glazes included pewter, orange, blue, green and treacle. These were applied to jugs, mugs, vases, pots, crocks, bowls and candlesticks, with some designs following the curvaceous lines of Art Nouveau. Wartime England saw the temporary closure of the Dicker Pottery which re-opened around 1946. Unfortunately, it never regained its pre-war favour and closed forever in the late 1950's.

The nearby Brickhurst Pottery which had been set up in 1952 by Fiona (a former Dicker employee) and Keith Richardson at Laughton produced items after the traditional Dicker style. The Richardsons suggest: 'they took up where Dicker left off' and for thirty years successfully ran Brickhurst until they retired in the 1980's. Norman Benjamin Bridges, who had worked at both Dicker and Brickhurst set up his own Merlin Pottery at Hellingly in 1963 and retired in the 1970's.

East Grinstead Pottery was founded in the mid-19th century by George Lynn, potter, builder, plasterer and stonemason. An advertisement indicated he could make everything necessary for the building trade such as drainpipes, tiles, bricks and chimney pots as well as flower, rhubarb and seakale pots and all household items in brown ware.

By the 1890's, the pottery had been taken over by a Henry Foster who expanded the range of brown ware and advertised – 'Items of any design and size could be made to order and in addition, there was a range of architectural ornaments'. When Henry Foster died in 1917 his three sons continued to run the business until the war.

Much of this pottery appears to be unmarked, but a few pieces are impressed with: - Henry Foster, East Grinstead Pottery Works.

Rye A ceramic industry of sorts has existed in Rye since the 13th century, yet Rye pottery only came to national attention under the auspices of the Mitchell family when they developed 'Sussex Rustic Ware' (1869 – 1920) at their Bellevue Works. From 1920 'Sussex Rustic Ware' was changed to 'Sussex Art Ware' and just before Bellevue closed in 1939 the name changed again to ' Old Rye Craft Pottery'.

In 1947 two brothers, Jack and Wally Cole, bought the dilapidated pottery in Ferry Road, Rye, re-christened their new venture, Rye Pottery and started to produce decorative items for the home at affordable prices. Their interpretations of those abstract styles, reminiscent of the 1950's and 1960's, brought a new look to ceramics and made Rye into an important pottery centre.

The history of Rye Pottery (neé Bellevue) began life in the 18th century as Cadborough Pottery just outside Rye, when the Cadborough Farm-cum-brickworks-cum-pottery was inherited by a Jeremiah Smith, Mayor of Rye and a man with many interests. Pottery was obviously not his main concern, for by 1840 he'd sold the business to one of his workers, William Mitchell.

Assisted by his two sons, Frederick and Henry, William continued to produce the customary items in brown ware but within ten years had included a fancy rustic ware.

This was largely due to Frederick Mitchell experimenting on certain pieces with applied decoration (sprigging) in the form of flowers, leaves, acorns and hops. It was obviously successful for Cadborough is listed in Kelly's Directories of 1866 as 'Manufacturers to HRH Prince of Wales and the Queen of Spain of the celebrated Brown and Fancy Rustic Ware'.

In 1869, Frederick left his father and brother to build his own house and pottery at Ferry Road in Rye, naming it Bellevue after the house at Cadborough. Working with potter William Watson, he concentrated on making fancy rustic ware, increasingly laden with sprigged embellishments. His work was highly regarded and examples of rustic ware can now be found in museums across the county. He also revived the traditional Sussex Pig (see Bottle Collecting).

When Frederick died in 1875, his widow Caroline, also an able potter, continued to run the business with the help of William Watson. Caroline introduced several classical lines of pottery that bore a resemblance to those of ancient Greece and proved

A pair of Bellevue Pottery candlesticks decorated with trailing green hops on a brown glaze. c.1890's. Anne of Cleves House Museum.

popular with the visitors to Rye. After her death in 1896 her nephew, Frederick Thomas Mitchell, took over the works officially, although it's thought the business had already passed to him a couple of years earlier. As well as some very fine miniatures, he continued to produce pieces with the ever-increasing applied decoration. These now included snakes, lizards and beetles, realistically crawling around jugs, mugs, urns and flowerpots. When Frederick died in 1920, his wife Edith kept the works going with help of employee, Bert Twort. In 1930 Bellevue was sold to a Mrs. Ella Mills but due to wartime blackout restrictions closed in 1939.

When Jack and Wally Cole bought Bellevue in 1947 they breathed new life into the old pottery. This involved new kilns, new shapes and eventually the new name, Rye Pottery. Shortly after the business had re-opened the brothers took on an apprentice by the name of David Sharp. Two more,

A 1950's Rye Pottery mug by David Sharp. 3¹/₂ ins (9 cms) high £24 - 28

Dennis Townsend and Ray Everett, followed in quick succession.

By 1960 each of these apprentices had left to pursue their own style and establish individual potteries in Rye. Of the three, David Sharp was probably the most versatile and innovative. Amongst other work his frequently exhibited range of model animals and birds are incredibly lifelike and unusual.

Meanwhile, Rye Pottery continued to expand and supply major outlets both in this country and abroad. One of their most sought after patterns was the 'cottage stripe' replaced in 1959 by the simpler 'candy stripe'. By the mid-60's, this as well as fifteen other different patterns were used on their wide range of tableware. Other pieces such as commemorative ware, vases, animals, chargers and lamps were also in demand. So too were the studio pieces, usually made by Wally.

Undoubtedly the 1960's and 1970's were the boom years for all the potteries in Rye – of which there were no less than seven or eight. Today there are still four. Wally Cole's son, Tarquin and his wife Biddy now run the eminently successful Rye Pottery, whilst the David Sharp Pottery, the Cinque Ports Pottery and Iden Pottery, whose origins began with the Cole brothers, continue to thrive.

Uckfield When the publican, Benjamin Ware took over the Uckfield brick, tile and pottery works in the mid-19th century, it was said he gave his men their wages with one hand and took them back with the other! A directory of 1886 lists Benjamin Ware and Son providing all kinds of building materials including sand, cement and clay. They also made glazed brown ware bread crocks, pitchers, pots, pans and some extremely interesting variegated ware. One or two examples of this curious 'stripey' pottery can be seen in Brighton Museum.

After Benjamin's death in 1910, his sons, Amos and William, continued to run the pottery. By now the works, one of the largest in Sussex, covered an extensive area with more than thirty cottages built to house employees.

Unlike others, Benjamin Ware and Son did not

c. 1900. A rare example of the variegated pottery produced by Benjamin Ware & Son, Uckfield. 5 ins. (13 cms) high. Private Collection.

close down during the war. Instead, they overcame blackout restrictions by means of building high brick walls around the kilns and placing corrugated iron sheets across the top. The business remained within the family but by the time it closed in 1970, it only produced horticultural items, tiles and bricks.

A 1970's pottery frog in cream and brown by David Sharp. 7 ins (18 cms) long. **£40 - £45.**

An early 20th century Dicker vase with three handles and a decorative green glaze. 3¹/₂ ins (9cms) high. **£90 - 100**

A Dicker Iron Lustre jug with typical Dicker twist to handle. c.!920. 10¹/₂ ins (27 cms) high. **£60 – 70**

An Iron Lustre Dicker vase. c.1920. 10 ins (25.5 cms) high. **£50 - 65**

A three handled Dicker in Iron Lustre. Marked UC&N. c.1915. 6¹/₂ ins (16.5 cms) high. **£58 - 68**

A 1950's Dicker lamp base with co-ordinating shade. Base 6¹/₂ ins (16.5 cms) high. **£45 - 55**

A triple Dicker vase in brown slipware. c.1920's. 5 ins (13 cms) high. **£145 - 165**

Two examples of Dicker's ochre coloured 'Treacleware'. c.1930's. Pot 3 ins (7.5 cms) high. Vase 2 ins (5 cms) high. **£25 – 35 each.**

c.1950's. A Dicker pewter glazed jug. 8¹/₂ ins (21 cms) high. **£35 - 45**

c. 1910. A blue glazed Dicker jug with slip decoration. Damaged. 6 ins (15 cms) high. **£38 - 45**

An unusual brown glazed Dicker vase with decorative slip. Marked UC&N. c. 1912. 7 ins (18cms) high. **£150 - 180**

A Dicker slipware mug. c.1900. Some damage to rim. 4¹/₂ ins (11.5 cms) high. **£45 - 50**

An early 20th century green glazed Dicker mug. 4¹/₂ ins (11.5 cms) high. **£90 - 100**

A Brickhurst Pottery tankard in a black lustre glaze, marked 'Brickhurst Pottery, Sussex' underside. **£12 - 15**

A 1920's Dicker bowl in a highly glazed combination of treacle and iron lustre. 8 ins (20 cms) diameter. **£65 - 75**

Two 1970's pewter glazed Merlin ware dishes. Impressed mark on underside 'Merlinware, Hailsham, Sussex'. 3¹/₂ ins (9 cms) diameter. **£12 – 15 each.**

c. 1970's. Three examples of pewter glazed miniatures from the Brickhurst Pottery at Laughton. 1 – 2 ins (3 – 5 cms) high. **£10 – 14 each**

A 1930's Dicker cold glazed orange pot. Some damage. 6¹/₂ ins (16.5 cms) high. **£40 - 50**

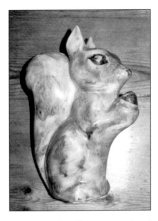

A David Sharp squirrel money box in blue. C. 1970. 8¹/₂ ins (21.5 cms) high. **£35 - 45**

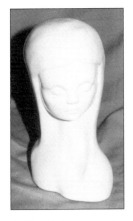

A David Sharp white glazed bust of the Madonna. Late 1960's. 6 ins (15 cms) high. **£65 - 75**

A blue glazed David Sharp money box in the form of a rabbit. **£60 - 68**

A David Sharp pottery cockerel in stylised green/blue floral pattern. c.1968. 10 ins (25 cms) long. **£45 – 55.**

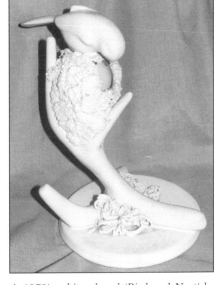

A 1970's white glazed 'Bird and Nest' by David Sharp. 9 ins (23 cms) high **£70 - 80**

David Sharp became well known for his animal pottery and this, amongst his other work, was on permanent exhibition in New York as well as various London Galleries. In 1966 he designed a chess set for the international tournament at Hastings commemorating the Battle of 1066.

A David Sharp floral patterned pig money box. Late 1970's. 5 ins (13cms) high. **£35 - 45**

c.1970's. A green/blue floral patterned hedgehog money box by David Sharp. 7¹/₂ ins (19 cms) long. **£35 - 45**

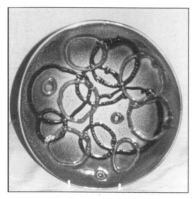

Ray Everett brown glazed plate with decorative green circles. c.1960's. 9¹/₂ ins (24 cms) diameter. **£28 - 32**

A copper glazed studio pottery vase by Ray Everett. c. 1960's. 10 ins (25.5 cms) high. **£40 – 50**

1960's Ray Everett pottery plate. 9¹/₂ ins (24 cms) diameter **£28 - 32**

An early 1960's Cinque Ports yellow mug. 7¹/₂ ins (19 cms) high. **£12 - 14**

A Ray Everett green glazed plant pot. 6 ins (15 cms) high. **£20 - 25**

A Cinque Ports yellow and white jug. c. 1960's. 15 ins (38 cms) high. **£25 - 30**

A 1980's Cinque Ports white pottery vase with blue decoration. 10 ins (25.5 cms) high. **£8 - 10**

Three 1980's Iden Pottery mugs inscribed in blue with name 'Alfriston'. 3 ins (7.5 cms) high. **£6 – 8 each**

A 1980's shallow dish from the Cinque Ports Pottery. 4 ins (10 cms) diameter. **£5 - 6**

A 1960's Rye Pottery coffee set decorated in black and white stripes, complete with six cups and saucers, a milk jug, sugar bowl and two pots. £350 - 450

Two Rye Pottery candy striped jugs. c.1960. 5 ins (13 cms) & 4 ins (10 cms) high. £35 – 45 each

c.1960. A Rye Pottery two-handled loving cup. 4 ins (10 cms) high. £120 – 140.

A Rye Pottery candy striped jug in black and white. c.1960. 5¹/₂ ins (14 cms) high. £42 - 48

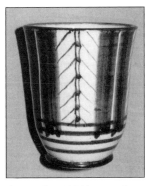

An early 1960's pot from Rye Pottery. 3¹/₂ ins (9 cms) high. £25 – 30

c.1958. A Rye Pottery jug. 9 ins (23 cms) high. £60 - 70

A Rye Pottery hedgehog. c. 1970's. 3 ins (7^1/$_2$ cms) long. **£23 - 28**

A blue and white Rye Pottery cat. 6 ins (15cms) high. **£40 - 45**

A textured Rye Pottery vase in green. c. 1950's 6 ins (15cms) high. **£60 - 70**

A Rye Pottery commemorative mug in manganese glaze and marked 'Sussex Martlets'. The sprigged crest showing six birds, from which the name Martlet is derived, is the Sussex coat of arms. c.1965. 3 ins (7^1/$_2$ cms) high. **£18 - 25**

A Rye Pottery engraved plate. 5 ins (13 cms) diameter. **£8 - 10**

A Rye Pottery mug in a black/white stripe. 4^1/$_2$ ins (11^1/$_2$ cms) high. **£20 - 24**

A white glazed pottery pitcher marked 'MH' 9¹/₂ ins (24 cms) high. **£5 - 6**

A 20th century white terracotta jug decorated with a blue/green/yellow floral pattern. From a pottery at Amberley. 8 ins (20 cms) high. **£5 - 6**

A late 20th century terracotta jug with a creamy glazed rim marked 'Gopsall'. 6¹/₂ ins (16.5 cms) high. **£5 - 6**

Terracotta pot marked 'Chappell' 5¹/₂ ins (14 cms) high. **£4 - 5**

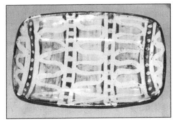

A Rodmell pottery dish. 8 ins (20 cms) long. **£4 - 5**

Please note that some of the collectables on this page are still being produced and the items shown reflect only their second-hand value.

A highly glazed white mug decorated with a blue and green fish. JCJ Pottery. 4 ins (10 cms) high **£1.50 – 2.00**

c. 1990's. A decorative stoneware wall pot from a pottery at Crawley. 5 ins (12.5 cms) high **£5 - 6**

Newick Pottery jug. 4¹/₂ ins (11.5 cms) high. **£8 - 10**

A textured Hastings Pottery plant pot. 6 ins (15 cms) high **£12 - 14**

SOUTHDOWN FARMING BYGONES

Primarily Sussex has always been an agricultural county. The invisible division between East and West, brought about for administrative reasons in 1888, did not suddenly change the geological structure either then or now. The chalk downland that begins at Beachy Head still continues unchanged across West Sussex, whose Wealden formations spread likewise into the upper regions of East Sussex. The rich pastures of the Sussex Levels have always provided ample grazing for cattle, whilst those lower downland slopes still offer acres of arable land. But today's concept of farming has altered dramatically.

A 19th century Sussex foot plough. £200 – 250.

A hundred years ago the flocks of sheep that roamed across the Downs far outweighed the current numbers. Sixty or more windmills once peppered the Sussex skyline, now only about fifteen remain most having been restored as visitor attractions. Harvesting used to be an occasion for entire villages to celebrate when completed.

Until the First World War the majority of farm machinery was horse-drawn. Hand tools were still in constant use, particularly on the very small farms. Here the seed would be sown with a hand seed drill. Hay was cut with a scythe, as was the corn although the more compact bagging hook was often used instead of a scythe. Potatoes were planted with a dibbler. Weeds taken out with dock lifters and hoes. Hedges were cut with

A 19th century hand seed drill with wooden spoked wheels. £100 - 120

bill hooks. Many of these tools were individually fashioned by the local blacksmith or the farmer himself. Latterly others were mass-produced. Some still bear the maker's mark although this may have worn away with use as tools were handed down from father to son.

The famous Pyecombe crook made by the Smith named Berry at the Pyecombe Forge in the late 19th century. Private Collection.

In general terms of farming, Sussex has always been associated with its famous Southdown Sheep whose wool was of considerable value. But as sheep farming broached new horizons, the traditional scene of the shepherd with his dog and flock had disappeared by 1960. The shepherd's crook, the smock, sheep shears, sheep bells, lanterns, the over-sized umbrella used as a shield from the wind, rain or sun, together with a few other tools of the trade, have now become collectors' items.

In the 1930's, the Pyecombe Forge, once noted for making the finest shepherd's crooks in the country, was lucky enough to find an alternative use for them – that of a crozier. On occasions, both the Bishops of Chichester and Lewes purchased the Pyecombe crooks as pastoral staffs.

Today at farm auctions many of the outdated items of 20th century machinery fetch little, principally because most would-be collectors simply do not have adequate storage. Therefore sadly, no matter how representative of rural history the equipment may be, pieces can

often be found poking from hedgerows, discarded, disintegrating and covered in years of debris.

To learn more about rural bygones, visit the farm or industrial museums. These will usually display various examples of seed drills, root cutters, hoists, scales, threshing and hay-making machinery, ploughs, traps, presses, harrows, grindstones and carts as well as a selection of smaller tools and devices.

A private collection of farming memorabilia. In the foreground, on the floor, the seed drill, a plunger butter churn and iron sack scales. On the wall, from left to right: thatchers' combs, a display of thatchers' tools, various choppers and hedge slashers, steelyards and turf lifters.

Wooden handled push hoe. c.1900. **£40 - 45**

Horse-drawn potato spinner. c.1910. This machine, as its name suggests, literally dug the potatoes from the ground then spun them out ready to be picked up. **£75 - 85**

Steelyards were made in various sizes to accommodate the average weight of the object. In use a steelyard was suspended and the item to be weighed hung from the double hook. The arm was then held horizontally and the pear shaped weight moved along the arm until the item was in balance.

Two horseshoes. 8 ins (20 cms) and 7 ins (18 cms) **£1 – 2 each**

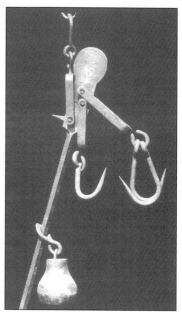

A steelyard. An early portable weighing machine. **£30 - 38**

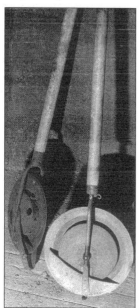

Two hand operated seed drills. **£20 – 25 each**

A leather bridle with brass embellishments. **£25 - 35**

Iron bridle rack. 11 ins (28 cms) high. **£20 - 24**

An iron turf lifter. 38 ins (96 cms) high. **£30 – 35.**

A branding iron. 18 ins (46 cms) long. **£4 – 5.**

A 19th century thatcher's comb which was used for dressing down the long straw thatch. 20 ins(51 cms) long. **£16 – 18.**

A 19th century oak butter churn. **£125 – 165.**

A sheep's bell. One of the many types used to indicate the whereabouts of the flock to the shepherd. **£12 – 14.**

A 19th century shepherd's crook. **£75 - 85**

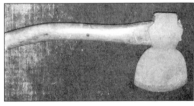

Trimming axe or chopper 18¹/₂ ins (47 cms) long. **£12 - 16**

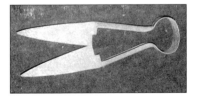

Sheep shears. 10¹/₂ ins (26 cms) long. **£5 – 6.**

A milk pan 8 ins (20 cms) diameter. **£8 – 9.**

A wooden hay turning fork. **£32 - 38**

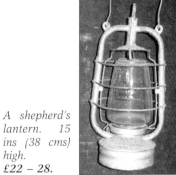

A shepherd's lantern. 15 ins (38 cms) high. **£22 – 28.**

SUSSEX BOOKS

There is little doubt that any hardback, paperback, or even a simple pamphlet on Sussex has a very long shelf life. The rolling downland, mellow villages, cliff top scenery and the bustling seaside towns sprinkled with royal connections, have inspired writers and poets alike. The historians have found plenty to write about too. The coming of the Romans in AD 43 with their grand villas at Bignor and Fishbourne, then subsequently the Saxons whose rustic settlements were dotted throughout Sussex from the 5th century onwards. Most famously there was William the Conqueror who landed at Pevensey to fight and win the battle of Hastings in 1066 and later, Simon de Montfort's victory against Henry III at the battle of Lewes in 1264. These are just some of the milestones in the much written web of Sussex history.

Since the last war, tourism has become big business – everywhere. To meet the needs of this booming industry there has been a surge of local interest books published and Sussex is no exception. Nowadays, the shelves of any bookshop will positively groan under the weight of books on the county's attractions, eccentricities and legends, books of old postcards or photographs, various guides, walks books, history and of course, books on the countryside itself.

Nevertheless, those pre-war years were not without their fair share of Sussex literature which, apart from being collectable, makes fascinating reading as the pace is somehow slower, the turn of phrase softer and the photographs a gentle sepia. That armchair traveller of the 1930's, Arthur Mee who, county by county, edited over forty volumes of 'The King's England' describes Sussex as being "a golden county, richly endowed by nature".

Most second-hand bookshops will carry a selection of old and not so old books on Sussex. Prices vary enormously and can depend on a number of different factors, such as the edition, author, age and probably most importantly, condition. An unsullied book with its jacket will obviously command a better price than the dog-eared version without. If you're thinking of starting a Sussex book collection, then it's worth visiting the library to get an idea of what's around. Boot fairs and jumble sales are excellent venues for a bargain – but do get there early.

'The King's England – Sussex' by Arthur Mee, published by Hodder & Stoughton in May 1937. Fifth impression 1950. **£9 - 10**

'Seaward Sussex' written by Eric Holmes with a hundred drawings by Mary M. Vigers. Published by Robert Scott in 1920. **£10 - 15**

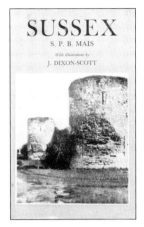

A part of a series of books on England, 'The Sussex Landscape' is by Peter Brandon and published by Hodder & Stoughton. First printed in 1974 and reprinted in 1977. **£6 - 7**

'Sussex River' – journeys along the banks of the Ouse from Seaford to Newhaven by Edna and Mac McCarthy. A paperback published by Lindel Organisation Ltd. c. 1970's. **£2.50 - 3**

'Sussex' by S P B Mais published by the Richards Press. First printed in 1929 and reprinted in 1937, 1941, 1950 and 1963. **£3.50 – 4.50**

'Romney Marsh' by Walter J C Murray published by Robert Hale Ltd. 1953. **£4 - 5**

'Sussex' by Esther Meynell and published by Robert Hale. 1947 **£7 - 8**

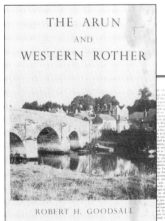

'The Arun and Western Rother' by Robert H Goodsall published by Constable and Company Ltd. in 1962. **£5 - 6**

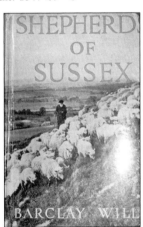

'Shepherds of Sussex' by Barclay Wills. **£6 - 7**

An illustrated guide to East Sussex. One of the A.B.C. paperback series of Crabtree Holiday Guides. This was first published by the Crabtree Press in 1950 with the 9th edition being in 1958. **£2.50 – 3.00**

The Penguin Guide to Sussex published by Penguin Books, 1957. **£3 - 4**

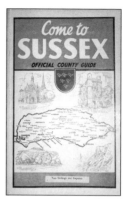

'Come to Sussex'. A paperback County Guide published by the County Associations Ltd., Berkeley Sq., London c. 1960's. **£3.50 – 4.00**

1938. 'Sussex'. The ninth edition of the Little Guides series first published by Methuen & Co. Ltd. in 1900. **£5 - 6**

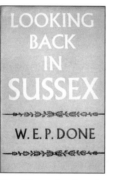

'Looking back in Sussex' by W.E.P. Done, published by Faber & Faber Ltd. 1953. **£2 – 2.50**

1904. A First Edition of "Highways and Byways in Sussex" by E.V. Lucas with illustrations by Frederick L. Griggs. Binding in poor condition. **£12 - £18.**

A tiny paperback guide to the History of Alfriston. Written by Florence A. Pagden and first published in 1899. Subsequent editions were in 1903, 1906 and 1917. **£3 - 4**

'Sussex' – Chambers Illustrated Guide and Souvenir by John Thorne MA, published by W&R Chambers. c. 1930 (in poor condition). **£3 - 4**

THE ROYAL SUSSEX REGIMENT

The complex history of The Royal Sussex Regiment spans two hundred and sixty five years and several titles. However, apart from its first Colonel, Arthur Chichester, whose surname matched that of the Sussex city, the Regiment had absolutely no connection with the county for the first eighty-six years of its existence.

In 1701, Arthur Chichester, 3rd Earl of Donegal and owner of large estates in Northern Ireland, raised the Regiment at his own expense in Belfast. In return for this and as a special mark of favour, King William III gave permission for orange facings to be used on the uniform. The Regiment's seniority number was '35' and it was then known as the Belfast Regiment. Unfortunately the first Colonel had little time to witness the successes and downfalls of his Regiment as he was killed fighting in Spain in 1706.

What became known as 'The Seven Years War' with France was declared in 1756 and accordingly the Regiment sailed to North America. Initially it acted as garrison of Fort William Henry before taking part in the famous Battles of Quebec in 1759. It was here the Regiment commandeered the white plumes worn by the French Regiment whom they had overwhelmed and put them in their own hats. Eventually the plume was incorporated in the regimental badge. The war ended in 1763 and the Regiment sailed home only to return to North America for the War of Independence some years later.

In 1782, George III added county titles to infantry regiments to aid recruitment and for some unknown reason, the Regiment then became the 35th (Dorsetshire) Regiment. It was during 1787 the first Sussex roots were established when a Charles Lennox joined the Regiment and recruited local

Badge and Colours of The 1st Battalion The Royal Sussex Regiment. Painted on vellum early 20th century. The Redoubt Fortress, Eastbourne.

men from his family estates within the county. By 1804 Lennox, later the 4th Duke of Richmond, had obtained Royal permission for the title 'Sussex' to be transferred from the 25th Regiment of Foot to the 35th, thus replacing 'Dorsetshire'.

After the Napoleonic Wars, which took place at the beginning of the 19th century, the Regiment served another long spell in the West Indies where their highly commendable achievements were duly recognised. On their return in 1832, King William IV conferred on the Regiment the title of 'Royal' and in acknowledgement the orange facings on the uniforms were replaced with the blue of a Royal Regiment.

Following the outbreak of the Indian Mutiny in 1857 the Regiment was moved to Calcutta and this resulted in close ties with the 107th (Bengal Infantry) Regiment. Sixteen years later a communal depot was created at Chichester and in 1881 the two Regiments were reconstituted to create the 1st Battalion and the 2nd Battalion The Royal Sussex Regiment.

1908 heralded more changes when a Territorial Army was formed from volunteers, the 4th Battalion in West Sussex and the 5th (Cinque Ports) in East Sussex. The Regiment served in both World Wars, 1914 – 18 and 1939 – 45. During the first, it lost 6,800 men and their names are recorded on the memorial panels in the Regimental Chapel of St. George in Chichester Cathedral. The names of those who fell in the second World War are recorded in a Memorial Book in the same Chapel.

In 1953, Her Majesty Queen Juliana of the Netherlands was appointed as the Regiment's Colonel-in-Chief. And finally in 1966, The Royal Sussex Regiment became a part of The Queen's Regiment together with The Queen's Own Buffs, The Queen's Royal Surrey Regiment, The Middlesex Regiment and The Royal Kent Regiment.

And whilst all the former traditions still continue here is a reminder of the Regiment's nostalgic marching song written by Mr Ward-Higgs of Bognor in 1907 and called 'Sussex by the Sea'.

"And when you go to Sussex,
Whoever you may be,
You may tell them all
That we stand or fall
For Sussex by the sea."

Those who require further information should note that a large collection of militaria detailing the history of The Royal Sussex Regiment can be seen at The Redoubt Fortress (Military Museum) Eastbourne. The Regimental archives are held in the West Sussex Records Office in Chichester. And based at Lewes, Wallis and Wallis are one of the leading militaria auctioneers in Britain. There are also several militaria specialists

A miniature drum inscribed "With many thanks for 3 years real help". Nov 1936. The Redoubt Fortress, Eastbourne.

who usually have a wide range of memorabilia on sale from their stalls in antique markets or at Fairs.

Shako – 1st Volunteer Royal Sussex Regiment. c.1869. £250 - 300

A plaster cast of the regimental badge of The Royal Sussex Regiment. Approx. 4 ins (10 cms) high. £12 - 18

Officer's full dress helmet. 2nd Regiment Sussex Rifle Volunteers. c. 1880. £350 - 400

Officer's waist belt clasp. 2nd Regiment Sussex Rifle Volunteers. c.1870 £120 - 150

A drum of The Royal Sussex Regiment with badge and Battle Honours. £500 - 600

Officer's waist belt clasp. Royal Sussex Regiment. c.1882 – 1900. £80 - 100

Large brass and enamel officer's badge of The Cinque Ports Battalion. *£60 - 80*

Royal Sussex Light Infantry Militia officer's cloth forage cap badge. c.1879. *£120 - 150*

1st Volunteer Battalion Royal Sussex Regiment badge. *£80 - 100*

Royal Sussex Regiment officer's cloth forage cap badge. c.1895. *£25 - 30*

Royal Sussex Regiment officer's cap badge. c.1947. *£80 - 150*

16th (Battle) Rifle Volunteers shako plate. c.1860. *£120 - 150*

10th (Chichester) Corps Sussex Rifle Volunteers officer's shoulder belt plate. c.1862 *£100 - 120*

35th (Royal Sussex) Regiment officer's shoulder belt plate. c.1850. *£120 - 170*

Cap badges, shoulder belt plates, clasps, pouch belt plates and helmet plates are made in a variety of metals including precious metal. This is reflected in the price but generally what is most important is the scarcity value. Beware of fakes, particularly common with badges.

Sweetheart brooches made in various metals and given by soldiers of The Royal Sussex Regiment to their loved ones whilst they were at war. £20 – 65 each.

A rare leather pouch of the 1st (Hastings) Corps, Cinque Ports Volunteer Rifles. c.1901 – 1908 £200 - 250

1914 – 1918 medals presented in a copper frame bearing a crest of The Royal Sussex Regiment. £35 - 45

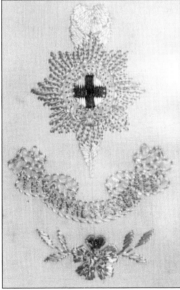

First World War postcard embroidered with the badge of The Royal Sussex Regiment. £10 - 15

A small Regimental tapestry, probably worked by soldiers convalescing after war. £60 - 70

WEALDEN IRON

Fifty years ago much of our ironwork ended up with the scrap merchants. Now it's found a well-deserved niche in the antiques market and prices start at a few pounds for, say, a simple ladle forged by a local blacksmith, to well over a thousand pounds for a handsomely burnished kitchen range or an exquisitely wrought iron garden seat made by the famous 18th century Coalbrookdale Works in Shropshire.

For the last two hundred years iron working has generally been associated with the Midlands and the North yet, somewhat surprisingly, until the end of the 17th century, the heart of England's iron industry lay in the Sussex Weald. These upper regions are located to the north of the South Downs and stretch from Petworth in the west to Northiam in the east.

The landscape is varied. Some of the hills are as high as the Downs themselves; the valleys are wooded and criss-crossed with streams. The villages have now become desirable hamlets with ribbon-like roads threading past white-washed cottages, tended gardens and grey stone churches. Today it's almost impossible to imagine this beautiful area as an industrial wilderness.

Although iron had been successfully worked in Sussex since Celtic times, under the influence of the Romans who appeared to keep their foundries mainly in the eastern part of the county, the industry positively

Examples of 18th and early 19th century Wealden ironwork.

flourished. This was primarily due to their harnessing masses of cheap labour to increase productivity. Yet by the time the Roman occupation of England had given way to that of the Saxons in 450 AD, the demand for Sussex iron had declined and many of the foundries had closed or operated on a reduced scale as other iron working sites were established further afield.

This downturn in the Wealden foundry business continued until the 13th century when the Crown suddenly requested from them a quantity of horseshoes, nails and arrows. This heralded the recovery for Sussex iron which, during medieval years, once again became a desirable and widespread commodity used for cannons, grave slabs, railings, fireplaces as well as most farm or household items. This also coincided with the more effective technique of smelting being introduced from France.

The height of the Wealden iron industry was undoubtedly during the 16th and 17th centuries when, to cope with the increased production, the number of ironworks escalated to around a hundred. Apart from ugly machinery, these were surrounded by dirty, dilapidated shacks built for the workers; the charcoal burners lived in huts in the forest where trees were being felled at such an alarming rate it caused national concern. Tributaries from the Rivers Brede, Ouse, Cuckmere, Rother, Arun and Adur had been dammed to make hammer ponds, whilst the rivers themselves were used for transporting iron downstream to waiting ships.

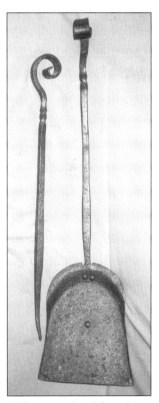

Fortunately for the desecrated Sussex landscape, coal was discovered in the Midlands and as it was cheaper to burn than wood, the foundries gradually moved northwards: the last to close was at Ashburnham in 1813. A few small foundries were re-established during the latter part of the 19th century, amongst them being the Phoenix Ironworks in Lewes, which continued to operate as a family business until 1950.

So, how many of the pieces seen in antique shops – or any other venue – are made from Wealden iron? Sadly, very few and those genuine examples that remain are usually found in museums, as are some of the pieces shown here. Others have been discovered in local auctions or Sussex smithies, where according to the blacksmith, they have been gathering dust since

19th century hand forged iron shovel and matching poker from the former smithy in Alfriston. 20 ins. (51 cms.) & 16 ins.(41 cms) £65 – 75 (2).

their grandfather's day.

In reference books, a lot of the household ironwork comes under the quaint term 'Kitchenalia' and whilst most of these items are now purely decorative, some have found an alternative use. Those little flat irons, which sell for about £15, make ideal door stops. The big iron pots that Great Aunt Daisy used for making jam fetch around £40 and look great filled with plants instead. Some of the old meat racks make good hat and coat hooks.

It often appears that the restoration of ironwork is rather a nebulous area and many shove a coat of black paint on the item in order to give it a quick face-lift. Try to resist this temptation. It makes iron look dull and lifeless and, more importantly, decreases the value. Nor should you lacquer iron that has been burnished. This gives an unrealistic glossy finish, which will eventually take on an odd yellowed appearance that requires professional cleaning once again. Instead, try two coats of wax polish and buff between each one. If, however, you prefer the traditional black glow, apply a coat of black lead polish (available from good ironmongers) with a brush onto the clean iron and work it into every crevice. Shine with a soft cloth.

A decorative example of ironwork made from old Wealden horseshoes. 30 ins (76 cms) diameter. **£65 – 75.**

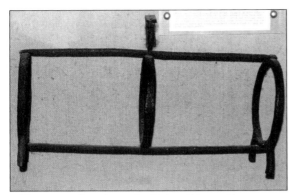

18th century clay pipe rack. 16 ins. (41 cms.) long.
£145 – 175.

An oval Victorian cooking pot. 15 ins. (38 cms.) wide.
£40 – 60.

*An 18th century iron toaster. The central'
bell' has six separate forks for toasting
bread and can slide up and down the stem
in order to gain the maximum benefit from
the fire. 32 ins. (81 cms.) high.* **£300 – 400.**

*Iron mortar. Used to crush herbs and spices
as well as medicinal powders. 6 ins (15 cms)
high.* **£45 – 55.**

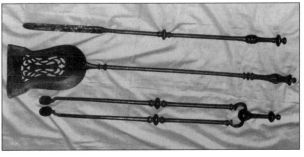

*Three 19th century fire irons. Poker and tongs 26 ins (66 cms).
Shovel 28 ins (71 cms).* **£200 – 225.**

19th century cast-iron candlestick. 11 ins (28 cms.) high. £75 – 85.

Three examples of 18th/19th c. pot hooks. £80 - 120 each.

Modern doorstop in the form of a cat. 13 ins. (33 cms.) high. £35 – 45.

A three-legged saucepan (sometimes known as a 'skillet') for standing on an open fire. 8 ins. (20 cms.) diameter. £30 – 40.

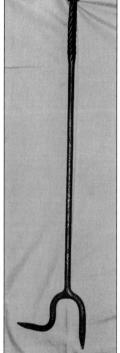

Circular iron trivet. 5¹/₂ ins. (14 cms.) diameter. £35 – 45.

Trivet cat. Made from six equal spokes, this 18th c. piece of ironwork provided a stand for pots as they were removed from the fire. 18 ins. (46 cms.) diameter. £120 – 140.

18th c. Iron log fork. 24 ins (61 cms.) long £80 – 100.

Weathervane illustrating the Blacksmith shoeing a horse. c.19th century. £200 – 250.

An 18th c. chimney crane. These often ornate items of ironwork were hung at the back of a fireplace to hang various cooking pots. The crane would then be swivelled across the fire when necessary. 38 ins. (96 cms.) high. £400 – 600.

Copy of a 19th century 'Idle Jennie' made by a blacksmith near Pulborough. Overall length 18 ins (46 cms). £75 – 85.

19th century iron kettle. £75 – 85.

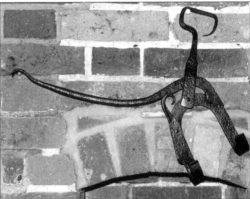

Did you know an 'Idle Jennie' was one of the names given to the curiously shaped piece of ironwork? This was because the 'handle' enabled the user to tilt the heavy kettle (which was hung on the bottom two hooks) without having to lift it away from the fire to make, for example, the tea.

ANTIQUE CENTRES & MARKETS

EAST SUSSEX

Battle Antique Centre. 91a High Street, Battle.	01424 773364
Brighton Flea Market. 31a Upper St. James Street, Kemp Town, Brighton.	01273 624006
Chateaubriand Antique Centre. High Street, Burwash.	01435 882535
Church Hill Antique Centre. 6, Station Street, Lewes.	01273 474842
Cornfield Antiques & Collectables. 18, Cornfield Terrace, Eastbourne.	01323 733345
Eastbourne Antiques Market. 80, Seaside, Eastbourne.	01323 642233
George Street Antique Centre. 47, George Street, Hastings.	01424 429339
Lewes Flea Market. 14a, Market Street, Lewes.	01273 480328
Needles Antique Centre. 15, Cinque Ports Street, Rye.	01797 225064
Newhaven Flea Market. 28, Southway, Newhaven.	01273 517207
Old Town Antiques Centre. 52, Ocklynge Road, Eastbourne.	01323 416016
Olinda House Antiques. Olinda House, South Street, Rotherfield.	01892 852609
Snoopers Paradise. 7-8, Kensington Gardens, Brighton.	01273 602558
Strand Quay Antiques. 1-2, The Strand, Rye.	01797 226790
The Barn Collectors Market. Church Lane, Seaford.	01323 890010
The Boxroom. Old Needlemakers, West Street, Lewes.	01273 471582
The Emporium Antiques Centre. 42, Cliffe High Street, Lewes.	01273 486866
The Emporium Antiques Centre Too. 24, High Street, Lewes.	01273 477979
The Enterprise Collectors Market. Enterprise Centre, Station Parade, Eastbourne.	01323 732690
Toad Hall Antiques Centre. 57, High Street, Heathfield.	01435 863535

WEST SUSSEX

Arundel Antiques Centre. 51, High Street, Arundel.   01903 882749

Barn Antiques at Country Gardens.
Stopham Road, Pulborough.   01798 874782

Great Grooms Antiques Centre.
Great Grooms, Parbrook, Billingshurst.   01403 786202

Horsham Antiques Centre. Park Place, Horsham.   01403 259181

Old House Antiques Centre.
Old House, Adversane, nr. Billingshurst.   01403 782186

Orchard Antique Market.
Old House, Adversane, nr. Billingshurst.   01403 783594

Old Town Antiques Centre.
The Old Town Hall, Market Square, Midhurst.   01730 817166

Petworth Antiques Market. East Street, Petworth.   01798 342073

Rocking Horse Antiques Market. 16, High Street, Ardingly.   01444 892205

Spongs Antique Centre. 102, High Street, Lindfield.   01444 487566

Stable Antiques. 46, West Street, Storrington.   01903 740555

Tarrant Street Antiques Centre.
Nineveh House, Tarrant Street, Arundel.   01903 884307

AUCTION ROOMS

EAST SUSSEX

Bonhams. 19, Palmeira Square, Hove.	01273 220000
Burstow & Hewitt. Lower Lake, Battle.	01424 772374
Country Auctions. East Ascent, St. Leonard's-on-Sea.	01424 420275
Eastbourne Auction Rooms. Finmere Road, Eastbourne.	01323 431444
Edgar Horn's. 46-50 South Street, Eastbourne.	01323 410419
Gorringe's inc. Julian Dawson. Terminus Road, Bexhill.	01424 212994
Gorringe's inc. Julian Dawson. 15, North Street, Lewes.	01273 472503
Gorringe's inc. Julian Dawson. Garden Street, Lewes.	01273 478221
Scarborough Perry Fine Arts. Hove Street, Hove.	01273 735266
Raymond Inman. Temple Street, Brighton.	01273 774777
Rye Auction Galleries. Rock Channel, Rye.	01797 222124
Wallis & Wallis. West Street, Lewes.	01273 480208
Watsons. The Market, Burwash Road, Heathfield.	01435 862132

WEST SUSSEX

Christies. North Street, Petworth.	01788 344440
Denhams. The Auction Galleries, Warnham.	01403 255699
Ellis & Son. 44-46 High Street, Worthing.	01903 288999
John Bellman. Wisborough Green, Billingshurst.	01403 700858
Peter Cheney. Western Road, Littlehampton.	01903 722264
Phillips. 49, London Road, Worthing.	01903 507060
Rupert Toovey & Co. Star Road, Partridge Green, Horsham.	01403 711744
Sotheby's South. Summers Place, Billingshurst.	01403 833500
Stride & Son. St. John's Street, Chichester.	01243 780207
Worthing Auction Galleries. Teville Gate, Worthing.	01903 205565

BIBLIOGRAPHY

The Badge Collectors Guide – Frank Setchfield

Stoneware Bottles – Derek Askey

Maritime Sussex – David Harries

A History of Sussex – J.A.Armstrong

Fountain Pens (US & UK) – Andreas Lambrou

Made in Sussex – Elizabeth Wright

Sussex Pottery – John Manwaring Baines

The Potteries of Rye – Carol Cashmore

A History of The Royal Sussex Regiment – G.P.Martineau

Curious Sussex – Mary Delorme

John Christie of Glyndebourne – Wilfrid Blunt

INDEX

THE AUTHOR

Sandy Hernu has spent most of her life in Sussex and has written, amongst other things, a number of books on both its history and countryside. Sandy also has a wealth of experience in the Antiques trade, having had antique shops in London and then, subsequently, Brighton for many years. Now she has combined her knowledge of Sussex and love of collectables to produce this first book on county memorabilia.

Together with her husband Jeffrey, Boxer Max and a cat called Ebenezer, Sandy lives in the delightful downland village of Alfriston. As well as her local interest books she has written the biography of the actor Desmond Llewelyn, best known as 'Q' of the James Bond films.

A regular contributor to various magazines on the subject of antiques, Sandy still finds time to combine her writing day with visiting auctions and fairs to keep abreast of current trends and prices as well as a bit of buying and selling.